# The Notary Survival Guide

Get It.
Read It.
Take It Everywhere You Go!

Daniel C. Jones, M.A., Ed., Notary Public

**The Notary Survival Guide**

Published by:
Daniel C. Jones
165 W. Hospitality Lane  Suite 10
San Bernardino, CA  92408
www.notaryclasses.com

 Publication data is available from the Library of Congress.

ISBN: 0-9776353-0-9

Printed and bound in the United States of America.

## ~ A Special Thanks ... ~

To my wife and kids, who put up with months of conversation about this book, most of which must have been incredibly tedious to them ... a special thanks.

To many of the instructors at www.notaryclasses.com who have assisted in the creation of this book with their ideas, opinions and thought-provoking discussions ... a special thanks.

To Carmen Chirilov, Cassandra Mason, Cheryl Elliott, Jeremiah Jones, Joan Bergstrom, Kelly Robertson, Sandy Bailey, Terri Garner and their assistants ... a special thanks.

To Andre Filip and Jeremiah Jones who created a book cover that I feel truly captures the intent of this book ... a special thanks.

To Sandy Bailey and Norma Gauthier who spent numerous hours crossing the t's and dotting the i's, only to have me go back and write another draft (so if there are still typos, it is my fault) ... a special thanks.

To Carol Ovalle, Francis Hernandez, Elizabeth Evans, Isabelle Cabral, Lisa Luna, Norma Gauthier, and Paola Caceres, who are all a pleasure to work beside ... a special thanks.

To the many notary publics who have set a high standard of excellence of public service ... a special thanks.

and

To you, for taking the time to read this book ... a special thanks!

# ~ Table of Contents ~

# ~ Foreword ~

I have been a notary public since 1994 and during that time have notarized thousands of documents. Since 2003, I have been fortunate enough to help many thousands of students pass the notary exam as a notary seminar instructor and the author and co-author of several notary-related curriculum programs.

The questions and answers in this publication reflect many of the questions asked by notaries over and over again. I believe that knowledge is a primary key of success in any field, and I hope your experience with this book brings you much success in whatever notary work you choose.

This book is based on 2005-2006 notary laws for the state of California. Each state has its own unique set of laws regarding notaries. Although I attempted to address questions relating to notaries across the country, it was by necessity that my focus was on California. Notaries from any state will surely benefit from many of the questions and answers in this book, but every notary must check with their own state laws for any deviation from this text. For example, many states do not allow the use of two credible witnesses, but since I know that California and Florida do, it was important to include that discussion.

This book is not intended to provide legal advice or legal assistance. It is an easy-to-read manual that will help you find notary-related answers quickly, while in the field or at home. All information contained within was researched, and although I am confident of the accuracy of each answer, I am not an attorney and reserve the right to correct any inaccuracies in future editions if necessary.

Best wishes in your notary career. I hope that my efforts in writing ***The Notary Survival Guide*** will help you to quickly achieve success.

*Daniel C. Jones*

# ~ Introduction ~

In writing this book, I had to manage a balance between those who read it from cover to cover and those who prefer to look up the questions and answers as each one became applicable or of interest.

For those of you who like to read cover to cover, please forgive the repetition of the content in some of the answers. I am sure you will understand that for the benefit of those who are selecting particular questions and answers, it was necessary to repeat some of the information. Hopefully the intent to balance was satisfactorily met.

For the sake of convenience, throughout the text in many instances I chose the commonly used phrase "notarizing the document." Notaries do not specifically notarize documents; they notarize the ***signatures*** on documents. However, since the term is so widely used among the general public and notaries alike, it is a reasonable assumption that not too many readers would take offense.

All notary practices and procedures explained within this text are based upon my personal experiences, research, and discussions with numerous longtime notary professionals. Not everyone will agree with all of the information or suggestions, but most will find a great deal of satisfaction in discovering possible solutions to some of the most common, yet perplexing notary questions we all face.

# ~ CHAPTER 1 ~
# After the Notary Exam

**Q. I have just taken my notary exam for California. What are my next steps?**

**A.** Almost everyone stresses out over taking exams. After helping many thousands of students pass their state notary exam, there are a few words of encouragement I want to pass along. First, the passing score in California is currently 70 percent or above. Even if you missed several questions, chances are high that you still passed. Of course, we all like to think of ourselves as above average and for good reason; we must be above average or we would not have taken the exam in the first place. Give yourself and those around you a break and forget about if for the rest of the day! Relax ... call a friend or better yet, go home and kiss someone you love.

Realize that passing the notary exam is only the first step of many during this exciting professional journey. Whether you get a score of 70 percent or 100 percent on your notary exam, there are things about the notary business you should learn that were not on the test. Reread your study guides and other books like this one. Quickly becoming as knowledgeable as possible will make a critical difference between success and slow going as a new mobile notary or a notary loan-signing specialist.

Now you are ready to take your next steps. Complete Step 2 as soon as possible, because this is one of the few steps for which your response can help the commission process along.

**Step 1:** After taking the California notary exam, you must wait seven to 10 business days for results. Your test results are sent to the mailing address you listed on your application. Exam results are also available online at https://notary.cps.ca.gov, but you still need to wait for seven to 10 business days from the day of the exam.

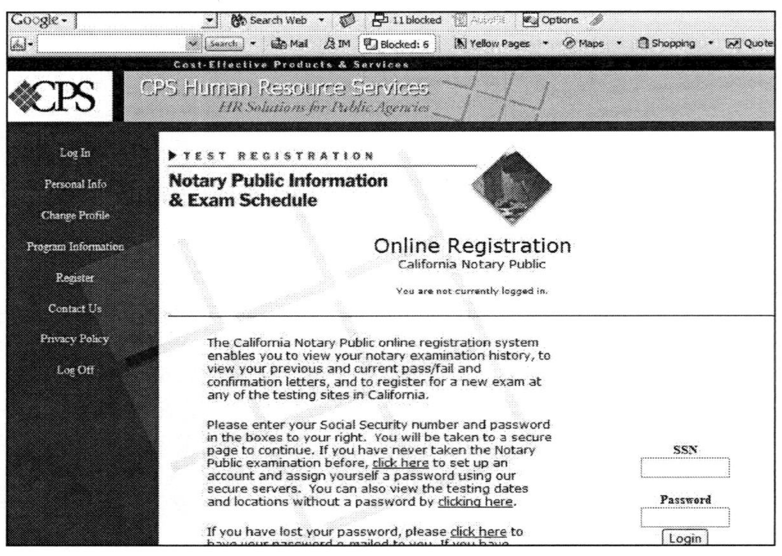

*Screen shot of the CPS Web site for California notary exams.*

To view your results online, log on and create an account on the CPS Web site by entering your Social Security number. If this is the first time you have taken a notary exam, you will need to obtain a password. Contact CPS Notary Services at (916) 263-3520 and press 5 for a representative if you have difficulties with this procedure.

**Step 2:** If your score is 70 percent or higher, congratulations; you passed! Now you must wait until you receive notification of passing by mail because it will also contain an application to begin your background check. You will have to make an appointment at a sheriff's office or third-party company for fingerprinting using a system called "Live Scan." A list of places to obtain a Live Scan is also sent to you by the secretary of state along with your notification. Fees do vary so check a few different providers.

Live Scan is a computerized system that takes a digital picture of your fingerprints and forwards them electronically to the secretary of state for a criminal background check. ***Make an appointment as soon as possible in order to expedite your commission process.***

**Step 3:** Assuming there is nothing in your background to warrant a denial of your commission, you will receive a Letter of Commission by mail within four to six weeks. If you have not received your commission within eight weeks from the day you completed your Live Scan, you might try calling the secretary of state's office at (916) 653-3595 to see if something has delayed your commission process. Do not call before eight weeks has passed because the staff will most likely be unable to assist you. Be patient, your commission will come.

**Step 4:** Once you receive your commission in the mail, you will need to purchase a $15,000 bond from an authorized surety company. The secretary of state provides a listing of authorized surety companies, so finding a bond is an easy step. Notary Rotary at (877) 349-6588 and Valley-Sierra Insurance at (916) 989-0900 are two resources I recommend for surety bonds.

You must now take your oath and file your bond with the County Clerk's office in the county named on your Letter of Commission. This county will be the one you named on your original notary application as the county of primary place of business. This is important because your county of residence may be different from your business county. For example, if you live in Los Angeles County but your notary office is in Orange County, you would file your oath and bond in Orange County. You can change your county of filing later if you like, but for now you must file within 30 days or your commission will be voided.

You may be thinking about becoming a notary loan-signing specialist and notarizing documents in multiple counties. Wherever you take your business orders for notary signings should be considered your primary county of business. If most orders are taken by fax or from home, then your primary county of business is also your home county, even though you will be notarizing documents in various counties.

Finding the address of the county clerk is a simple Internet search. An easy-to-use site for finding business addresses and phone numbers is www.superpages.com.

*Screen shot of www.superpages.com search for county clerk.*

Sometimes the company that issues your bond will file your bond and oath on your behalf using a limited power of attorney. Check with the company first. However, remember that if you rely on the bond company to file it for you and it is not done within 30 days of the date of your Letter of Commission, the commission is void and you will have to reapply all over again. Your exam results will be good for one year, so if you do have to reapply, do so within a year.

To take your oath and file the bond in person, find the notary section in the county clerk's office and present the bond documents to the staff. You will also complete the oath of office at that time. The filing fee for both the oath and bond should be around $30. Do not notarize any documents before you complete the filing of your oath and bond, because you may be held liable for any losses derived from an illegally notarized document. Notaries are not fully commissioned until the oath and bond are on file with the county clerk.

You also have the option of taking your oath before a notary. Along with your Letter of Commission, you will receive a printed oath which needs to be signed.

Normally, this is the document you would take to the County Clerk's office. Take the oath to a notary and after notarization, mail both the oath and the evidence of bonding to the county clerk's office. The county clerk must receive this within the 30 days or your commission will be voided.

**Step 5:** Your Letter of Commission, which is sometimes referred to as a Certificate of Commission, will have a gold seal and will provide a four-year term of commission and your commission number. You should also receive an authorization to have two notary seals manufactured. You will need to send the original authorization (not a copy) to the seal manufacturer of your choice. A listing of authorized seal manufacturers are provided to you by the secretary of state with your Letter of Commission, so finding a seal manufacturer will be no problem.

Please note that if at any time during your four-year term you lose or damage your seal, you must notify the secretary of state by certified mail. At the same time you may request another authorization for a replacement seal.

**Step 6:** Now that you are a commissioned notary public you are ready to begin notarizing. ***Before you do, read the rest of this book so you will know what to do when you begin.*** It takes six to eight weeks for the entire commissioning process to finalize and you should use this time to become familiar with as many notary processes as you can. Too many notaries start marketing their services and make mistakes, because they have forgotten what they learned for the exam or they never learned something important, such as how to notarize the signature of a power of attorney. This book covers a wide variety of situations and becoming familiar with them will be critical to your success as a notary public.

Begin marketing your services by telling everyone you know that you are a notary public. Think about all the people you know in your state. Each one of us is probably acquainted with more than a hundred other people including friends, relatives, co-workers, neighbors and so on. Each of those persons is most likely also acquainted with more than a hundred other people. You have a potential client base of thousands but no one will know if you do not tell them. Almost everyone needs a notary sooner or later. Word of mouth is always the best form of advertising, not to mention one of the only free forms of advertising.

Finally, follow the steps listed in the final chapter of this book, "How Do I Make Money?," in order to maximize your success. If you are thinking about offering your services as a loan signer, become certified as quickly as you can.

**Q. How much should a bond cost?**

**A.** At the time of this printing (2005), a bond of $15,000 should cost between $28 to $35 for all four years. If you are being quoted more than that price, it is too much. The bond must be obtained from a surety company who is authorized to sell bonds for California.

Not all states require bonds and some require less than $15,000. Of course, if you are a notary outside of California, you will need to become familiar with the laws of your particular state. Many states also require bonding prior to completing your commission process as a notary.

**Q. Is a bond the same thing as Errors and Omissions (E&O) liability insurance?**

**A.** Some new notaries are curious about whether they should purchase a bond greater than $15,000. Bonding companies will not offer a notary a bond for more than the legally required amount since a bond for more than $15,000 is not necessary nor does it provide the notary with additional benefits.

Remember that the bond does not provide protection for you as the notary. It is meant to provide protection to the general public in the event that you are successfully sued for illegal or negligent actions, and you do not have sufficient assets to pay the award.

The plaintiff (the person who files the complaint or charge with the court against you) can collect the bond on file in such cases, but you are then obligated to the bonding company for the entire amount taken.

Additionally, if the award is over $15,000, the plaintiff may file a judgment for the award, and other means may be used to force collection.

For this reason, almost every active notary purchases at least $15,000 of Errors and Omissions (E&O) liability insurance. If you have purchased E&O insurance and are sued, the E&O policy will pay the award. You will not be obligated to reimburse the E&O company as you would the bonding company. Many notaries will purchase more than $15,000 of E&O even though E&O insurance is not required by legislation.

**Q. How much should Errors and Omissions (E&O) liability insurance cost?**

**A.** At the time of this printing (2005), a $15,000 policy should cost around $45 for all four years. Be aware that many companies, including some of the largest ones, sell Errors and Omissions (E&O) liability insurance policies with yearly premiums. Shop around and you will save a lot of money. Do not settle for yearly premiums, as the policy will cost much more. You also might consider policies higher than $15,000. Notary Rotary (877) 349-6588 and Valley-Sierra Insurance at (916) 989-0900 are two recommended resources for E&O insurance.

**Q. I am a California notary and have already filed my $15,000 bond with the county clerk. Why do some companies require that I also purchase Errors and Omissions (E&O) liability insurance before I can work with them if it is not legally required?**

**A.** Remember that a notary is personally held liable for illegal or negligent notary acts which result in financial losses. There is no limit for liability. The notary can be held personally liable for any amount of loss if he or she is found responsible.

Suppose, for example, a plaintiff can prove a loss of $50,000, and the court finds the notary to be liable because of illegal or negligent actions. The notary's $15,000 bond on file with the county clerk will be forfeited to the plaintiff, and the notary will also have to pay the additional $35,000 from whatever resources he or she has. Additionally, the surety company that forfeited the $15,000 bond will also sue the notary to recover their money.

Although working as a notary can put you at financial risk, few notaries will ever face lawsuits especially considering the number of documents notarized daily. This is why the Errors and Omissions (E&O) liability insurance is so inexpensive. With so few claims against notaries, the risk for the insurance companies is minimal. Notaries who blatantly falsify documents or their own notary work are at the highest risk of being sued, or even ending up with criminal charges.

The greatest majority of notaries will never be sued even when they have made a mistake on a document. Not all notaries escape liability, so considering this fact, and that E&O liability insurance is so inexpensive, any notary offering services to a bank, mortgage company, signing company, title company, or lender will undoubtedly be required to have E&O insurance.

Just about every company to whom you advertise your services will require you to send them a copy of your E&O policy. It is simply a small cost of doing business and even more important, an inexpensive stress reliever.

**Q. How much Errors and Omissions (E&O) liability insurance is recommended?**

**A.** Errors and Omissions (E&O) liability insurance is so important that the recommendation is to purchase a $100,000 policy if you can afford it. At the very minimum, you should purchase a $15,000 policy in order to cover your bond should it ever be necessary. Remember to check prices before you buy because they vary widely. Some companies only offer $15,000, but there are quite a few offering $100,000 policies. If you are having trouble finding them, go online and search for "$100,000 notary policies."

You should not consider notarizing any document without at least a $15,000 E&O policy. These policies are around $45 for all four years.

**Q. What happens if the bond is awarded as a result of a legal suit against the notary?**

**A.** If the bond is awarded to a plaintiff as a result of a lawsuit, and you do not have the financial ability to pay, the surety company who put up the bond on your behalf will be required to pay the award up to a maximum of $15,000. Should the award be higher than $15,000, you will be responsible directly for the balance.

As stated previously, the surety bond is not the same thing as insurance. ***The surety bond protects the public and E&O liability insurance protects you.*** Without E&O insurance, any amount paid by the surety company on your behalf will be subject to collection from you. The surety company may be required to pay up to $15,000 because you purchased their bond, but that does not release any of your personal liabilities. Once the surety company has paid the plaintiff, you will receive notification from the surety company requiring reimbursement of the entire amount paid on your behalf. Protect yourself ... buy an E&O policy.

**Q. What are the chances of being sued?**

**A.** In general, a notary who uses common sense and does not engage in illegal acts as a notary will enjoy a career free from litigation. Notaries who are unethical are much more likely to have charges filed and, of course, subsequent legal consequences. Of course, everyone can make an unintentional error, so a notary who has Errors and Omissions (E&O) liability insurance is protected for such times. Even unintentional errors rarely culminate in litigation against the notary.

E&O insurance for notaries is very inexpensive because insurance companies experience very few losses from notaries. The chances of a good notary being sued are minimal, and with E&O insurance in place, a negligible consideration.

Even though it is unlikely you will ever be sued as a notary, you need to always exercise caution. Never give legal advice and never suggest to a client that the document he or she is signing may not be in his or her best interest.

As a notary, you are actually providing a service on behalf of the state; hence, you are a public servant. Unless you are also an attorney, your role as a notary is always neutral. Check identification carefully and if you are not fully satisfied that it proves the identity of the document signer, seek an additional identification source or decline the notarization.

Be sure your journal records contain all of the necessary information as required. You can add additional information in your journal if you find it necessary. For example, if a client satisfactorily proves identification, but asks questions you find suspicious, note your suspicions in the journal.

A notary may receive a subpoena to testify in court concerning a particular signing. Having notes in your journal can help you recall the details about the signer, especially if he or she raised suspicions during the signing. Be careful on this point. You are not permitted to reject the notarization just because someone looks suspicious to you. As long as the document is complete, identification is proven, and the signer will pay for your services, you must notarize the document as requested.

If someone does name you in a lawsuit, the court will require evidence that you did something illegal or were negligent in fulfilling your duties, and your actions cost the plaintiff money. Protect yourself by establishing excellent notary habits. Become as familiar as possible with notary laws in your state and keep good records.

**Q. What is the difference between a jurat stamp and a notary stamp? Do I need to purchase both?**

**A.** Sometimes new notaries are confused between a notary stamp (often called a notary seal) and a jurat stamp. These are two different stamps used for two completely different purposes.

The notary stamp is used when notarizing a document regardless of the document type or title. A notary stamp in California will have the name of the notary, the state seal, the commission number and expiration date of the notary. The notary stamp also indicates the county where his or her bond is on file with the county clerk.

A jurat stamp is very different. Documents that require specific jurat wording by the state often lack that wording. For example, in California, beginning in 2005, all jurats must include wording regarding the proper identification of the document signer. Since jurat wording prior to 2005 did not require this information, many preprinted forms have obsolete wording.

To rectify this issue, notaries can use a jurat stamp which has the correct wording. If there is room on a document requiring the corrected jurat verbiage, a jurat stamp is very convenient and completely acceptable.

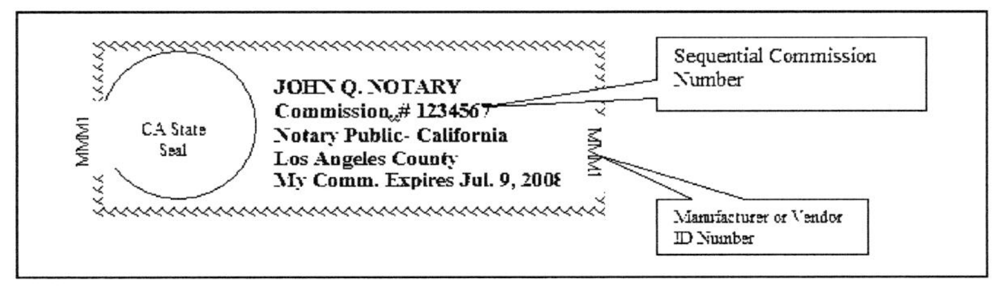


*Example of a California notary stamp or seal.*

Any document you notarize in California must have a clear, photographically reproducible notary stamp that you must purchase.

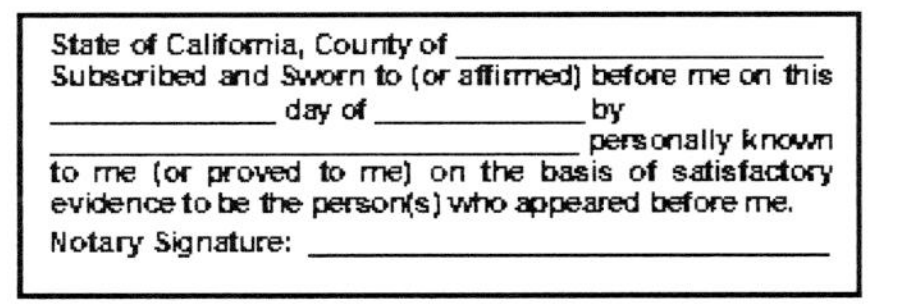

State of California, County of ____________________
Subscribed and Sworn to (or affirmed) before me on this ____________ day of ____________ by ______________________________ personally known to me (or proved to me) on the basis of satisfactory evidence to be the person(s) who appeared before me.
Notary Signature: ______________________________

*Example of a California 2005 jurat stamp.*

While you are not required to purchase a jurat stamp, without one you will be forced to add a separate jurat form containing the proper wording when notarizing documents in California without correct jurat verbiage. I suggest you purchase the jurat stamp along with your notary stamp. The cost is minimal and the convenience is huge. You may need jurat forms anyway if documents do not have enough room for a jurat stamp, but it still will be very useful throughout your career as a notary.

**Q. I am a first-time notary and have just recently taken my notary exam. Is there anything I can do while waiting for my commission?**

**A.** Once you have submitted your fingerprints via Live Scan, there is not much you can do to expedite your commission. However, many applicants take this time to attend a loan-signing certification program. Clearly the notaries who make the most money are certified loan signers. The best use of your time while waiting for your commission is to go through a loan-signing certification process.

The best programs should cover the following:

- Review of basic notary legislation;
- Loan-signing protocol and procedure;
- Marketing techniques of successful loan signers;
- Review of the most common loan-signing documents;
- Mock loan signings.

Because of the quality of the program and all of the additional benefits associated with it, the loan-signing class offered by www.notaryclasses.com is one of the most comprehensive you can find. As a co-author of this program, great care was taken in providing the notary with loan-signing protocol and ideas for successful marketing. Registration for this program can be done online at www.notaryclasses.com.

After the seminar you will take an exam online, in which you have two attempts to pass with a score of 80 percent. Both of these attempts are included in the price of the seminar. Once you have passed the exam, you will provide a digital image of yourself for a photo-identification card identifying you as a Certified Notary Signing Agent and a member of the Association of Professional Notaries and Certified Signing Agents (APN & CSA).

Of course, you will not receive your certification until after you receive your notary commission, but if you take this step in the interim, you will be ready to market yourself as soon as your certification and photo ID are delivered.

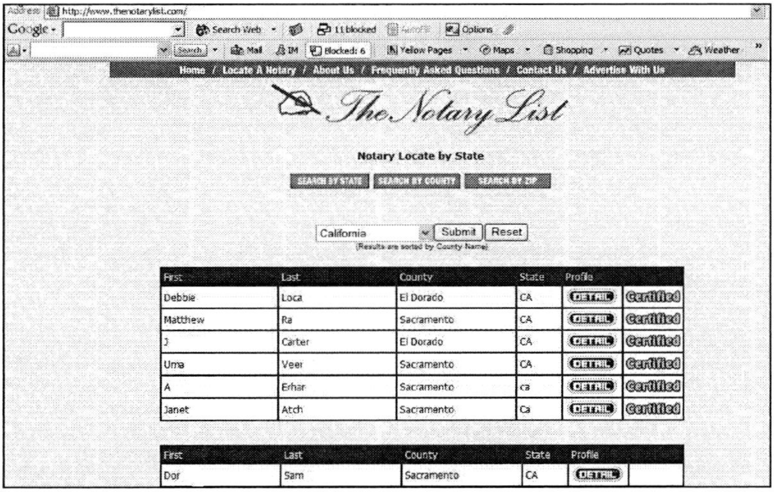

Home / Locate A Notary / About Us / Frequently Asked Questions / Contact Us / Advertise With Us

The Notary List

Notary Locate by State

SEARCH BY STATE | SEARCH BY COUNTY | SEARCH BY ZIP

California Submit Reset

(Results are sorted by County Name)

| First | Last | County | State | Profile | |
|---|---|---|---|---|---|
| Debbie | Loca | El Dorado | CA | DETAIL | Certified |
| Matthew | Ra | Sacramento | CA | DETAIL | Certified |
| J | Carter | El Dorado | CA | DETAIL | Certified |
| Uma | Veer | Sacramento | CA | DETAIL | Certified |
| A | Erhar | Sacramento | ca | DETAIL | Certified |
| Janet | Atch | Sacramento | Ca | DETAIL | Certified |

| First | Last | County | State | Profile | |
|---|---|---|---|---|---|
| Dor | Sam | Sacramento | CA | DETAIL | |

*Thenotarylist.com is a free notary registry for www.notaryclasses.com loan-signing students. The listing is free for one year. Listing on these sites increases your market exposure as a notary and loan signer.*

**Q. What should I do if I fail the exam the first time?**

**A.** If you do not pass the exam the first time, retake it until you do pass. You must wait until the following calendar month, but you may take the exam as many times as you need.

**Step 1:** Go to https://notary.cps.ca.gov and select a city or county convenient to you. You will see a listing of dates and locations of upcoming notary testing sites. Click on the one that interests you and complete the registration information.

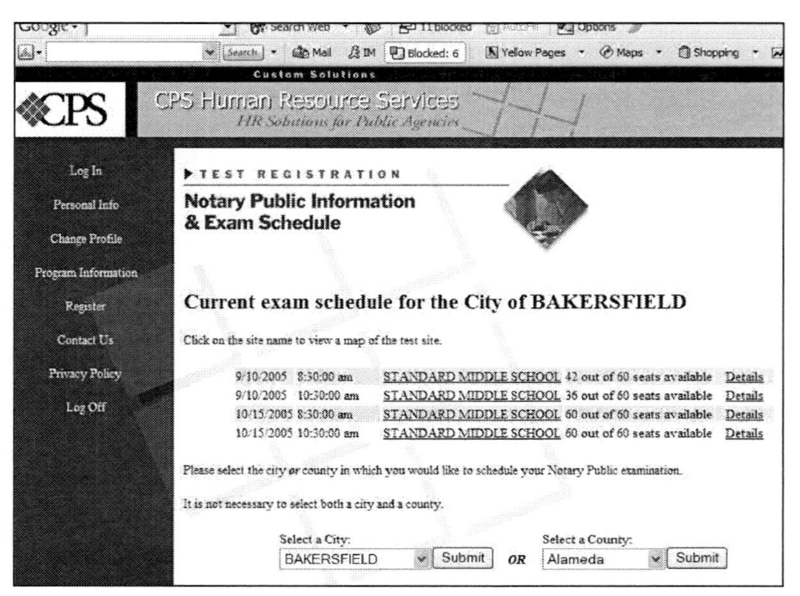


*Screen shot for checking California notary exam schedules.*

**Step 2: *Read this book*** and study the text materials provided during your class. If you took a home-study course, review the text carefully. In addition, you may want to download and study the California ***2005 Notary Public Handbook***. California students can go to: http://www.ss.ca.gov/business/notary/notary.htm and follow the links to the state handbook. Applicants from other states can review the requirements for their particular state's retesting procedures.

**Step 3:** Show up early at your exam site to eliminate stress. Be sure to take your identification, a copy of your fail letter from your first attempt, and a check or money order for $20 payable to the secretary of state. Take a Number 2 pencil with you as well, in case the CPS proctors run out at the testing site.

**Step 4:** Take your time on the test. Do not rush and be sure to read every question and answer carefully. Be aware of all-inclusive words like "in every case," "never" or "always." If you are not sure of an answer, skip it and come back later. Check your answers when you are finished and be the last person to leave the testing site. Many of the questions are worded in a convoluted manner; verify and reverify the meaning before you are satisfied. This takes time and effort, but doing so will minimize simple errors and your score should be much higher than before.

**Step 5:** Wait seven to 10 business days for your results. Then follow the steps mentioned in the beginning of this chapter.

# ~ CHAPTER 2 ~
# Renewing or Changing Commissions

**Q. I am a notary in California. How do I comply with the new 2005 regulations regarding mandatory education in order to renew my commission?**

**A.** Effective July 1, 2005, any person in California seeking commission or recommission as a notary is required to submit a proof of completion of an approved six-hour notary education course along with the commission application. Most notary classes or seminars in California currently offer the state testing immediately following the class.

Once you have taken the approved six-hour course, subsequent recommissions will require only a three-hour refresher course. The educational requirement affects all notary applicants regardless of how many previous terms they have held.

**PROOF OF COMPLETION**

THIS IS TO CERTIFY THAT

________________________________________
(Name of notary public applicant or notary public attending the approved seminar)

HAS SATISFACTORILY COMPLETED THE FOLLOWING 6-HOUR COURSE OF STUDY AS REQUIRED BY THE STATE OF CALIFORNIA, SECRETARY OF STATE FOR NOTARY PUBLIC EDUCATIONAL REQUIREMENTS

**HOW TO PASS CALIFORNIA'S NOTARY EXAM**

ON ____________________.

Identifying information

Type of identifying information ______________

Identifying number ______________

State or country of issuance ______________

Expiration date ______________

Vendor Name:
NOTARYCLASSES.COM
Vendor Number:

Name of instructor:

____________________
Authorized Signature:

____________________

Date of Issuance ______________

(A) Proof of completion shall be valid for a period of two (2) years from the date of issuance
(B) Proof of completion must be attached to the notary public application when submitted to Secretary of State

*Proof of Completion certificate.*

**Q. My commission is expiring in about six months. What should I do to recommission?**

**A.** Notaries seeking another term may not take the exam sooner than six months prior to the expiration of their current commission. If you are within the six-month period, register for a notary class or seminar.

Once you have taken the exam, follow the steps given in Chapter 1. You will not need to resubmit fingerprints. Any recommissioning notary who has not allowed more than six months to lapse after the expiration date of his or her commission does not have to resubmit fingerprints.

As long as you take the exam at least six weeks before your commission expires, the secretary of state will usually do everything possible to ensure you will not have a lapse in your commission. If you take your exam really early, you may need to wait a little longer for your letter of commission. It is usually sent to you just before the expiration of your current commission.

California notaries should be aware that most notaries are finding the current exams much more difficult to pass. Regardless of how many terms you have served, without adequate preparation, you may be surprised at your scores. It is advisable to take your exam early so if you do not pass the first time, you will not have a lapse in your commission.

**Q. Do I need to send my notary seal and journals to the secretary of state when my commission expires?**

**A.** When your commission expires, you must destroy your notary seal. If you are not planning to seek a recommission, you must turn in your journals to the county clerk where your bond and oath are on file within 30 days from the expiration of your current commission. The same is true if you resign your commission early.

Do not send your seal or journals to the secretary of state unless you receive a letter requiring you to do so. If you are recommissioning, secure your old journals in a locked area under your control. It is not necessary to begin a new journal between commissions if the current one is not full.

A word of caution to recommissioning notaries: sometimes notaries forget that each commissioning term requires a refiling of the oath and bond. Every new four-year term requires a new notary seal, a new bond, and a new oath. Notarizing documents without filing a new oath and bond is illegal and can subject you to serious consequences.

**Q. I obtained my notary commission as a requirement of my job with a governmental public office. If I leave my job, do I also have to resign my commission?**

**A.** If you are a California notary and you have obtained your commission to fulfill a job-related requirement, and your position required you to notarize documents for a public school system, a governmental public office or the military, you must resign your commission upon termination of your job.

This does not mean that every employee who becomes a notary at the request of his or her employer is required to resign the commission upon termination of his or her job. In fact quite the contrary. A notary commission belongs to the notary regardless of who paid the fees to obtain the commission. It remains with the notary until resignation or expiration.

Even those notaries who happen to work for a public school system or public governmental offices but hold their commission through personal efforts or choices may also retain their commission upon resignation or termination of their employment.

Notaries who are in the military, however, will resign their commission upon exiting the military or transferring to another military installation.

**Q. My commission is expiring and I do not want to renew my commission because I am moving out of state. Do I need to notify the secretary of state since I am moving?**

**A.** In California, if you move during your term or if you change your primary place of business, you are required to notify the secretary of state by certified mail within 30 days. Failure to comply with this requirement could subject your commission to revocation or suspension.

The secretary of state's office may need to quickly locate you in the event of an investigation or other communication relative to your duties. If you do not keep them informed of your new location, valuable time can be lost. Be sure to notify the secretary of state if you move or change your job and had listed your job address as your primary place of business.

If your commission is expiring and you are not renewing your commission, there is no legal requirement to notify the secretary of state of an address change. However, be sure to comply with the requirement of submitting your journals to the county clerk within 30 days. Failure to comply could result in a misdemeanor charge.

**Q. I have recently married. How do I change the name on my commission to reflect my married name?**

**A.** Many notaries change their name within the term of their commission due to marriage or divorce. To notify the secretary of state for California notaries, go to http://ss.ca.gov/business/notary/notary_formsfees.htm

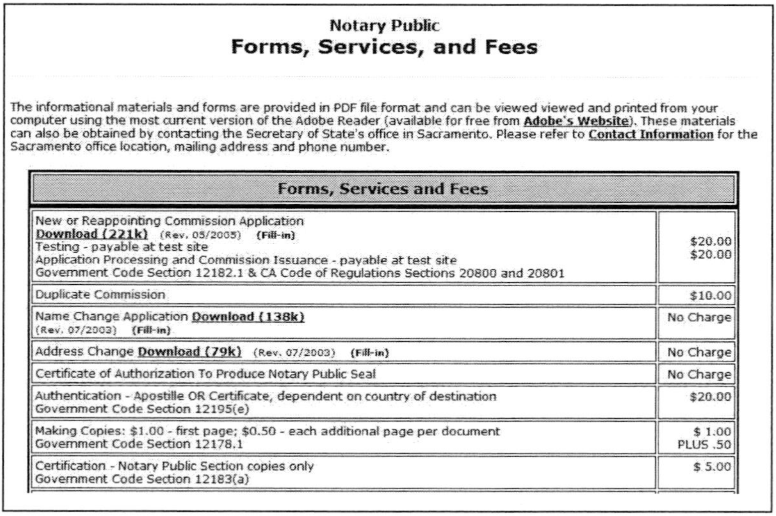

Notary Public

**Forms, Services, and Fees**

The informational materials and forms are provided in PDF file format and can be viewed viewed and printed from your computer using the most current version of the Adobe Reader (available for free from **Adobe's Website**). These materials can also be obtained by contacting the Secretary of State's office in Sacramento. Please refer to **Contact Information** for the Sacramento office location, mailing address and phone number.

| Forms, Services and Fees | |
|---|---|
| New or Reappointing Commission Application<br>**Download (221k)** (Rev. 05/2005) **(Fill-in)**<br>Testing - payable at test site<br>Application Processing and Commission Issuance - payable at test site<br>Government Code Section 12182.1 & CA Code of Regulations Sections 20800 and 20801 | $20.00<br>$20.00 |
| Duplicate Commission | $10.00 |
| Name Change Application **Download (138k)**<br>(Rev. 07/2003) **(Fill-in)** | No Charge |
| Address Change **Download (79k)** (Rev. 07/2003) **(Fill-in)** | No Charge |
| Certificate of Authorization To Produce Notary Public Seal | No Charge |
| Authentication - Apostille OR Certificate, dependent on country of destination<br>Government Code Section 12195(e) | $20.00 |
| Making Copies: $1.00 - first page; $0.50 - each additional page per document<br>Government Code Section 12178.1 | $ 1.00<br>PLUS .50 |
| Certification - Notary Public Section copies only<br>Government Code Section 12183(a) | $ 5.00 |

*Screen shot for the California secretary of state Web site containing forms such as a name change application.*

You can download the proper form and forward it to the secretary of state. Remember that you will also need to request authorization to have a new notary seal manufactured with your new name.

You will receive a new Letter of Commission reflecting your new name, but your commission number and expiration date remain the same. You are not obtaining a new commission, just changing your commission name.

It will be necessary to also change the name on your bond through an amendment with the company who issued it. Once you receive this amended bond, you will file it and take a new oath with the county clerk within 30 days of receiving the new commission. Be sure to file with the county clerk before you begin using your new notary seal.

# ~ CHAPTER 3 ~
# Conflicts of Interest

**Q. I am a real estate agent and have been asked to notarize documents for my clients. Am I allowed to do this?**

**A.** A great deal of confusion surrounds conflict of interest laws regarding notary publics. California notary legislation specifically addresses many questionable areas surrounding this issue.

The following excerpt from the secretary of state ***2005 Notary Public Handbook*** is reprinted for your convenience. The notary, in the example given here, is acting in the capacity of an agent for his or her client. Assuming the agent is not named specifically as a party to the transaction (grantor or grantee, for example), notarizing the documents while working for the client in the capacity of an agent is permissible under this legislation.

***§ 8224. Conflict of interest; financial or beneficial interest in transaction; exceptions***

*... For purposes of this section [real estate property], a notary public has no direct financial or beneficial interest in a transaction where the notary public acts in the capacity of an agent, employee, insurer, attorney, escrow, or lender for a person having a direct financial or beneficial interest in the transaction. (California Notary Public Handbook, 2005.)*

To reiterate, if the agent is also the named as the seller, mortgager or otherwise named as a party to the transaction, the agent then assumes a dual role and as a party to the transaction, would not be permitted to notarize any documents associated with the transaction.

For example, if the agent owns the property, he or she is engaging in a dual role as the real estate agent and the seller. He or she would have a beneficial interest in the documents being notarized.

**Q. Both my spouse and I own a business and there are often documents that require notarization. Can I notarize my husband's or wife's signature for these documents?**

**A.** The following reprinting of § 8224 states if the notary is named individually as a principal to the transaction, the notary may not notarize the document. In this case, however, the notary is the spouse of the individual who has a direct beneficial interest in the transaction.

***§ 8224. Conflict of interest; financial or beneficial interest in transaction; exceptions***

*A notary public who has a direct financial or beneficial interest in a transaction shall not perform any notarial act in connection with such transaction. For purposes of this section, a notary public has a direct financial or beneficial interest in a transaction if the notary public:*

*(a) With respect to a financial transaction, is named, individually, as a principal to the transaction.*

*(b) With respect to real property, is named, individually, as a grantor, grantee, mortgagor, mortgagee, trustor, trustee, beneficiary, vendor, vendee, lessor, or lessee, to the transaction.*

The legislation seems a little less clear in this case, however the California ***2005 Notary Public Handbook*** interprets this section by stating the following:

*A notary public is not prohibited from notarizing for* ***relatives****, unless doing so would provide a direct financial or beneficial interest to the notary public. (Government Code section 8224) With California's community property law, care should be exercised if notarizing for a spouse. (California Notary Public Handbook, 2005.)*

The question is whether or not the spouse, as the notary, directly benefits from the transaction. Our question, as stated, indicates that both the husband and wife are named as business owners and consequently, both parties have a direct beneficial or financial interest in the document. In this case, the spouse ***should not*** notarize the document.

The matter becomes a bit more complex, however if the husband owns the business as a sole proprietor. In this situation, the wife is not named as owner but an employee (or simply a third-party notary). Whether the wife, acting as a notary directly benefits from notarizing forms for her husband's business may now become a matter for the courts to interpret should a disagreement ensue.

Similarly, this issue of conflict of interest is duplicated when both spouses are named as officers of a corporation. While it is permissible for a notary who is an employee having a direct beneficial interest in the corporation to notarize documents, the notary may still not directly benefit from the transaction.

If a notary is also a stockholder in a corporation, then the notary should not notarize documents for that corporation since the document would presumably benefit the notary directly. If both the husband and wife are stockholders of the corporation, as is usually the case, neither one should notarize documents for the corporation. Corporate officers who are not also corporate stockholders are permitted to notarize documents for the corporation as long as they are not named within the document as a principal.

**Q. My landlord is selling the office building and has requested that I notarize the sales documents. I am not named in any of the documents and will not have a financial benefit resulting from the sale. Am I allowed to notarize these documents?**

**A.** If you have read the previous sections in this chapter, you will remember seeing California legislation prohibiting a notary from notarizing any documents associated with a sale of a property if the notary is leasing the same property.

***§ 8224. Conflict of interest; financial or beneficial interest in transaction; exceptions***

*A notary public who has a direct financial or beneficial interest in a transaction shall not perform any notarial act in connection with such transaction. For purposes of this section, a notary public has a direct financial or beneficial interest in a transaction if the notary public:*

*(a) With respect to a financial transaction, is named, individually, as a principal to the transaction.*
*(b) With respect to real property, is named, individually, as a grantor, grantee, mortgagor, mortgagee, trustor, trustee, beneficiary, vendor, vendee, lessor, or lessee, to the transaction. For purposes of this section, a notary public has no direct financial or beneficial interest in a transaction where the notary public acts in the capacity of an agent, employee, insurer, attorney, escrow, or lender for a person having a direct financial or beneficial interest in the transaction.*

This does not mean that you cannot notarize other types of documents for your landlord. You are also not prohibited from notarizing documents with respect to the sale of the office building if you are an employee of the lessee, as long as you are not named as a principal within the lease or in the documents to be notarized.

**Q. Can I notarize a document for my spouse or relative?**

**A.** As previously stated, notary legislation in California does permit a notary to notarize a document for a spouse or relative so long as the notary does not have a direct beneficial or financial interest in the document.

*Government Code § 8224. A notary public is not prohibited from notarizing for* ***relatives****, unless doing so would provide a direct financial or beneficial interest to the notary public. With California's community property law, care should be exercised if notarizing for a spouse. (California Notary Public Handbook, 2005.)*

The key is determining whether or not the notary has a direct beneficial or financial interest. Clearly, if the notary is named on a grant deed as a grantee or a grantor, he or she should not notarize the document.

Suppose the grant deed is between the parents of a spouse and the spouse? Depending on how title is taken, an argument may be made for the spouse who is a notary not having a direct beneficial interest.

For example, suppose the property is granted to the spouse as "a married man as sole and separate property," as is often the case with such transfers. Suppose the wife, in this case, notarizes the document, assuming no beneficial interest in the document since she is excluded from ownership through title. This act may still prove risky especially if other siblings of the spouse decide to contest the transfer. Frankly, who needs the legal battles? If you are concerned about a possible conflict of interest, take the document to another notary.

If you are a notary in another state, check your own state laws before notarizing for a spouse or relative, as some states do not permit this practice.

# ~ CHAPTER 4 ~
# Acknowledgments and Jurats

**Q. What is the difference between an acknowledgment and a jurat?**

**A.** Without question, the two most common duties completed by a notary are "performing an acknowledgment" and "administering a jurat." Each one serves a specific purpose, and it is important for a notary to know exactly which one to complete and why.

**Acknowledgments**

Performing an acknowledgment means that the signer of the document:

1. Personally appears before the notary at the time of notarization.
2. Acknowledges to the notary that the signature already on the document is his or her signature or the notary personally witnesses the signing of the document by the person requesting notary services.
3. That the signer was properly identified by the notary as the person named within the document.

In California, an essential part of the acknowledgment process is that the signer is also acknowledging that he or she is executing the document in his or her authorized capacity. This is critical because it means that if someone is signing a document as CEO of a company or a partner of a Limited Partnership, the signer does not need to prove that capacity to the notary. The very act of signing the document is enough to acknowledge to the notary that he or she is signing in an authorized capacity.

Some states require the notary to verify the authorized capacity of a document signer, but not in California. California notaries must be aware that since some states require the notary to verify the authorized capacity of the signer, acknowledgment wording for those states will be different than in California.

The proper wording for an acknowledgment in California is:

State of ____________ }
County of ____________ } ss.

On ____________ before me, ____________
(Date) (Notary)

personally appeared ____________
Signer(s)

personally known to me (or proved to me on the basis of satisfactory evidence) to be the person(s) whose name(s) is/are subscribed to the within instrument and acknowledged to me that he/she/they executed the same in his/her/their authorized capacity(ies), and that by his/her/their signature(s) on the instrument the person(s), or the entity upon behalf of which the person(s) acted, executed the instrument.

Be aware that the signer is claiming his or her own "authorized capacity." Effective January 2006, all acknowledgements taken in California must have this wording in its exact form, unless the document will be recorded in another state. Documents to be recorded in a state outside of California often will have different acknowledgement wording which is acceptable for that state.

This is the only instance when a notary in California may use modified acknowledgment wording and only if that wording does not require the California notary to do something against California state law.

As we saw previously, since some states require the notary to verify the signer's authorized capacity, it is possible a document may be brought or sent to a notary in California which has been drawn in that state, but is illegal for a California notary to notarize.

STATE OF ____________

COUNTY OF ____________

On this ________ day of ______________, ____________, before me, the undersigned, a Notary Public in and for the State of ______________, duly commissioned and sworn personally appeared ________________________________ **to me known or proved to me** to be the ______________________ of ______________________, the corporation that executed the foregoing instrument and acknowledged the said instrument to be the free and voluntary act of and deed of said corporation, for the uses and purposes therein.

Notice the section that requires the notary to either know or have proven to him or her the signer's authorized capacity. It is illegal for a notary in California to comply with a request from another state if it requires the notary to perform any action specifically prohibited by California notary legislation. Completing this acknowledgment is a perfect example of such an illegal request. Instead of filling out this acknowledgment wording, the notary in California must use a form called a "California All-Purpose Acknowledgment" which has the correct wording.

We will see later that the signer of a jurat must sign the document in the presence of the notary, but if a document requires an acknowledgment and was signed prior to presentation to the notary, it does not need to be re-signed. The notary, however, must ask the document signer to acknowledge that the signature on the document is indeed his or hers.

You can see where the term acknowledgment comes from. The signer is acknowledging to the notary that the signature on the document represents the same person named within the document and is also acknowledging to the notary that he or she is signing with his or her authorized capacity.

**CALIFORNIA ALL-PURPOSE**
**CERTIFICATE OF ACKNOWLEDGMENT**

State of ______________ }
County of ______________ } ss.

On ______________ before me, ______________
(Date) (Notary)

personally appeared ______________
Signer(s)

personally known to me (or proved to me on the basis of satisfactory evidence) to be the person(s) whose name(s) is/are subscribed to the within instrument and acknowledged to me that he/she/they executed the same in his/her/their authorized capacity(ies), and that by his/her/their signature(s) on the instrument the person(s), or the entity upon behalf of which the person(s) acted, executed the instrument.

Stamp clear impression of notary seal above.

WITNESS my hand and official seal.

______________
Notary's Signature

OPTIONAL INFORMATION

| CAPACITY CLAIMED BY THE SIGNER | DESCRIPTION OF THE ATTACHED |
|---|---|
| ☐ Individual (s) | ______________ |
| ☐ Corporate Officer | **Title of Document** |
| ______________ (Title) | ______________ **Number of Pages** |
| ☐ Partner(s) | ______________ |
| ☐ Attorney-in-Fact | **Document Date** |
| ☐ Trustee(s) | ______________ |
| ☐ Other ______________ | **Other Information** |

*The California All-Purpose Acknowledgment, also referred to as a "loose certificate."*

Finally, with acknowledgment verbiage, we find an implied acknowledgment of the signer's intent to execute the document. This means that the document signer is tacitly stating that he or she wishes to cause the stipulations of the document to be carried out.

For example, if the document is a grant deed, the grantor(s) would desire, with his or her signature(s), to grant the property named to a grantee(s). The signature is notarized and sets the stipulations of the property transfer in motion. Notice that nowhere in the acknowledgment verbiage is the signer required to swear or affirm the truthfulness of the document.

## Jurats

A jurat differs from an acknowledgment in that it requires the document signer to swear to or affirm the veracity of the contents within the document. An acknowledgment does not require the signer to swear that the document represents the truth, but the purpose of a jurat is to:

1. Guarantee that the document signer personally appeared in front of the notary at the time of notarization.
2. Guarantee the document signer took an oath regarding the truthfulness of the document.
3. Require that the document signer sign the document in front of the notary. If the document was signed previously and the notarization requires a jurat, the document signer must re-sign the document in front of the notary after he or she completes the verbal oath.
4. Require the notary to administer the oath or affirmation to the document signer, prior to signature.
5. Requires the notary properly identify the document signer at the time of notarization.

Prior to January 1, 2005, jurats did not require the signer to be identified in California. This means most documents with jurat verbiage preprinted on the form will be incorrect. The correct verbiage for jurats in California is:

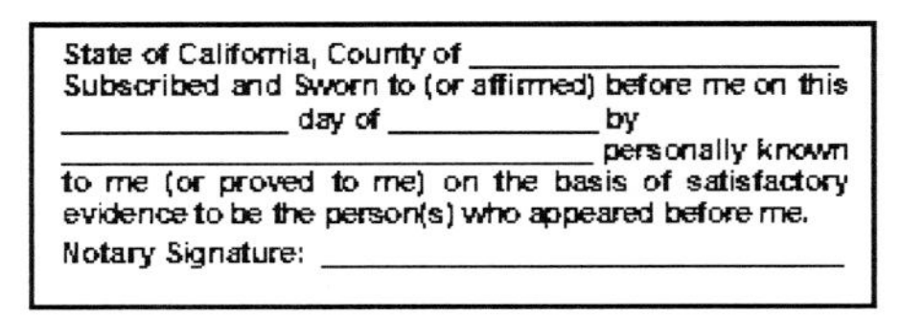

State of California, County of ____________
Subscribed and Sworn to (or affirmed) before me on this ________ day of ________ by ____________ personally known to me (or proved to me) on the basis of satisfactory evidence to be the person(s) who appeared before me.
Notary Signature: ____________

If you have a document that requires a jurat and it either has no jurat verbiage preprinted on it or omits any of the words as printed above, you will need to either use a jurat stamp to correct the verbiage or attach a jurat form for California. You can obtain a free jurat form, if needed, at www.notaryclasses.com.

**Q. How do I know whether to use an acknowledgment or a jurat?**

**A.** Virtually every document you notarize will require either an acknowledgment or a jurat. In most instances, the document will have either acknowledgment or jurat verbiage preprinted on the form so you will know immediately what is required. If a document has acknowledgment wording preprinted, you must assume, unless instructed otherwise by your client or his or her attorney, that you are expected to complete an acknowledgment. If it has preprinted jurat verbiage, you can assume that you are to complete a jurat.

Forms with preprinted verbiage indicate which notary act to perform, but sometimes you may encounter documents that should require a jurat but have acknowledgment verbiage instead. For example, suppose someone had his or her home burglarized and the insurance company requires a notarized statement regarding the missing items. After listing the items on the form, there is another statement that requires the signer to swear to the truthfulness of the statements within the document.

As the notary, you might assume that the notary act requested is a jurat, yet in most cases, it is preprinted acknowledgment verbiage. Since non-attorney notaries are not permitted to give legal advice or legal assistance, the notary must comply with the request of the client regarding which notary act to complete. Of course, the client rarely will know if he or she needs an acknowledgment or a jurat, but if you are presented a form with one or the other already printed, you are safe to complete that notary act, unless instructed otherwise.

There are many forms presented for notarization without preprinted notary wording. What is to be done in such cases? You can ask the signer if he or she requires an acknowledgment or jurat, but once again, the chances of him or her knowing which notary act is required is remote.

As a notary, unless you are also an attorney, you may not advise the client regarding which notary act is to be completed; the client must tell you. Notaries are supposed to ask the client to contact the document originators if he or she does not know which notary act to perform, but this solution is quite often, impractical.

Suppose, as in our previous example of the home burglary, the client brings you a letter regarding the missing items with a statement swearing that the information listed within is true, but the letter does not have any notary wording printed for you. You know that such a statement would most likely require a jurat; however, the insurance company may have wanted an acknowledgment instead.

In such instances, if the document originator cannot be reached, some clients request that both notary acts be performed. Remember that you are not permitted to advise the client and the decision must be his or hers alone.

Sometimes it is the client who drafts the document for notarization. For example, you may be handed a Permission for a Minor to Accompany an Adult letter drafted by the client, that lacks notary verbiage. In this case, you might explain that completing a jurat means verifying that the document signer has sworn that the contents of the document are true, and an acknowledgment is intended to make sure the signer is signing in his or her authorized capacity and that he or she wishes to execute the stipulations of the document. Once again, be careful not to advise the client. Instead, let the client select which notary act he or she prefers.

This sounds much more complicated than it is in reality. Ninety percent of the time the client will have no idea what is required and will want your advice. Just explain that you are not allowed to make the decision for him or her, and the signer will choose very quickly. One word of caution: many notaries simply produce an acknowledgment, thus in effect, making the decision for the client. It is doubtful that complaints have ever been filed against a notary for doing so. Remember, however, that you are violating notary law if you do not allow the client to decide which notary act to complete.

**Q. How do I fill out an acknowledgment properly?**

**A.** Chances are as a brand-new notary, the first acknowledgment you will ever complete for a client will be many weeks after you have studied notary law and passed the notary exam. You may feel apprehension with the first couple of acknowledgments, and for good reason. If an acknowledgment is not filled out correctly and the document is to be recorded, the county recorder will probably not accept it. The document will need to be re-notarized properly, and your client could be upset with you.

Filling out an acknowledgment is quite a simple process; but, like anything else, familiarity is the key.

State of ______________ }
County of ______________ } ss.

On ______________ before me, ______________
(Date) (Notary)

personally appeared ______________
Signer(s)

personally known to me (or proved to me on the basis of satisfactory evidence) to be the person(s) whose name(s) is/are subscribed to the within instrument and acknowledged to me that he/she/they executed the same in his/her/their authorized capacity(ies), and that by his/her/their signature(s) on the instrument the person(s), or the entity upon behalf of which the person(s) acted, executed the instrument.

Begin by completing the venue section which is denoted by the words "State of______" and "County of_____." The venue is always the state and county where the notarization takes place. If you are notarizing a document in Sacramento County, California, then regardless of where the document has been drawn, where it is going to be recorded, or where your commission is held, you must notate California as the state and Sacramento as the county, since this is where the document signer personally appeared before you at the time of notarization.

Sometimes the notary section will be pre-filled by an escrow company or other third party, and quite often the venue will be wrong. Simply cross out the wrong information and write in the correct state and county. ***The notary wording is the only section on any document you may change by hand without prior permission from the originator of the document.***

The date is always the date the notary acknowledgment is completed. If a pretyped date is incorrect, once again, cross out and change it.

Complete your name as the notary, and in the next section, print the name of the person(s) who appear before you at the time of notarization.

You will now need to indicate whether the signer(s) was/were known to you, or if he/she/they proved his/her/their identity to you with satisfactory evidence such as a state driver's license. In this case, let's assume the signer used his or her driver's license for identification. There is no precise method required, so simply underlining the word "proved" or underlining that phrase is sufficient. Some notaries also cross out the inapplicable phrase, which in this case would be "personally known to me."

Completing the next part is critical but unfortunately, too many notaries ignore this section. Reading through the following acknowledgment wording, you will note the pronoun forms he/she/they and the singular/plural forms for various terms.

> ...to be the person(s) whose name(s) is/are subscribed to the within instrument and acknowledged to me that he/she/they executed the same in his/her/their authorized capacity(ies), and that by his/her/their signature(s) on the instrument the person(s), or the entity upon behalf of which the person(s) acted, executed the instrument.

The notary must properly indicate the correct forms by either circling them or crossing out the incorrect forms. For example, if notarizing for John Doe alone, the acknowledgment would be completed as follows:

> STATE OF CA
>
> COUNTY OF SAN BERNARDINO
>
> On July 14, 2005 before me, Daniel C. Jones, Notary Public, personally appeared John Doe, ~~personally known to me~~ (or proved to me on the basis of satisfactory evidence) to be the person~~(s)~~ whose name~~(s)~~ is/~~are~~ subscribed to the within instrument and acknowledged to me that he/~~she/they~~ executed the same in his/~~her/their~~ authorized capacity~~(ies)~~, and that by his/~~her/their~~ signature~~(s)~~ on the instrument the person~~(s)~~, or the entity upon behalf of which the person~~(s)~~ acted, executed the instrument.

Now sign the acknowledgment and place your notary seal somewhere close to your signature. Be sure that your seal has a clear impression because if it is smeared or smudged, the county recorder may not record the document. Some notaries like to also use an embossed notary stamp, sometimes referred to as a "notary press stamp." The embossed stamp is not required and does not substitute for the notary seal in California. However, some states are still using the press stamp, so check with your state laws regarding its use.

The press stamp or embosser can be used along with the notary seal as a way of adding additional security for the notary. In our digital age, a notary seal can be easily duplicated and illegally used. While the notary is not held liable in such fraudulent circumstances, using a notary press stamp may add an additional layer of protection for any document the notary completes.

Sometimes you are presented documents for notarization that do not have enough room for your seal. The acknowledgment wording may be preprinted on the form, but there is no place for your seal around the verbiage or your signature. Never place your seal on the header of the page or somewhere far off from the notarized verbiage just because there may be enough room for it there.

In this case, fill out the acknowledgment verbiage on the form, but do not place your seal over any typed or written text. If you do not have enough room on the page with the document signer's signature, attach a separate acknowledgment form to the document. You will need to fill out this acknowledgment form and place your seal on this page. Remember, you may never place your notary seal on any page that does not have proper notary verbiage, so do not place your notary seal on a blank page or on the reverse side of the document.

**Q. How do I fill out a jurat properly?**

**A.** The second most-often completed notary act is known as "administering a jurat." The form completed for this act is called a "jurat." Remember, the essential difference between a jurat and an acknowledgment is that a jurat is used to indicate the document signer has sworn to the notary that the contents of the document are true to the best of his or her knowledge.

Filling out a jurat once again requires designation of the venue. The venue is always the state and county where the document signer personally appeared before the notary, took the oath (or affirmation), and signed the document in front of the notary. Remember that with an acknowledgment, the document signer does not need to sign the document in front of the notary; he or she simply acknowledges that the signature is indeed his or hers.

A jurat, however, always requires the document signer to sign the document in front of the notary and always after he or she has replied affirmatively to the oath or affirmation given by the notary.

The following is the proper jurat verbiage for California to be used on all jurats after January 1, 2005.

State of____

County of ________________

Subscribed and Sworn to (or affirmed) before me this ____ day of ___________, 20 ___ by ____________________________ personally known (or proved to me) on the basis of satisfactory evidence to be the person(s) who appeared before me.

___________________

Notary Signature

The date always indicates the day the document signer completed the jurat process of swearing the oath and signing the document.

When you print the name of the person(s) who appear(s) before you at the time of notarization, it is important the name is correctly spelled. Print the person's name in the blank space following the word "by," since it was this person who took the oath and signed the document. As with acknowledgments, the name you print on the jurat should be consistent with the name within the document which should also be the same as the signature.

> State of CA
>
> County of Los Angeles
>
> Subscribed and Sworn to (or affirmed) before me this 12th day of March, 2005 by John Doe ~~personally known~~ (or proved to me) on the basis of satisfactory evidence to be the person~~(s)~~ who appeared before me.
>
> ________________________ (Notary Seal)
>
> Notary Signature

If you personally know the document signer, either circle the words "personally known" or cross out the words "proved to me on the basis of satisfactory evidence." Otherwise, cross off "personally known."

Sign the jurat and place your notary seal next to your signature. If you do not have enough room on the document for your notary seal, you will need to either attach a jurat form, or, using a blank piece of paper, use your jurat stamp and notary seal and then attach that to the document. A jurat stamp with the correct verbiage for jurats can either be applied to the document itself (if it does not have the correct jurat verbiage), or on a separate page, as long as it is attached to the original document.

You should never give your client completed and sealed loose jurats or acknowledgment forms that have not been attached to the applicable document. Always attach them and, even though law does not require it, you should also always note information about the source document. Remember to never place your notary seal on any paper or document without notary verbiage.

Most states do not currently require the notary to identify the signer of a jurat, but most notaries ask for identification anyway. Prior to 2005, a California notary was not required to identify the document signer, but that changed with a new law effective January 2005. Now all jurats completed in California must include verbiage indicating the document signer was personally known or was properly identified by the notary. Since most forms with jurats have been printed using pre-2005 notary wording, if you are a notary in California, you must use the different wording in order to comply with this law. A county recorder in California will not record a document with an incorrect jurat.

Subscribed and Sworn to before me

this ______________ day of __________. 19 ____________

_______________________________________________
Signature

Notary Public Commissioned for said County and State

*Incorrect pre-2005 jurat wording.*

If a form has pre-2005 jurat wording, cross out the incorrect jurat wording with one diagonal line and use your jurat stamp, or complete and attach a loose jurat form to the document. The notary seal must be placed on the loose jurat certificate since it is illegal for a notary seal to be placed on any document not containing proper notary wording.

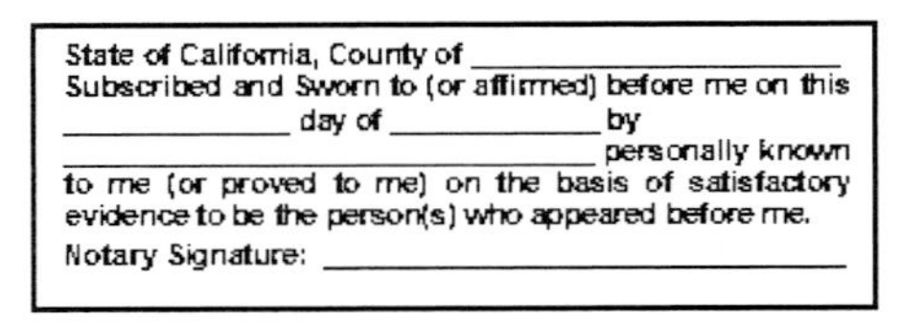
State of California, County of ____________________
Subscribed and Sworn to (or affirmed) before me on this
____________ day of ____________ by
______________________________ personally known
to me (or proved to me) on the basis of satisfactory evidence to be the person(s) who appeared before me.
Notary Signature: ____________________

*Correct jurat wording in California beginning January 2005.*

**Q. What is an "affiant"?**

**A.** If you have read the previous sections on the differences between acknowledgments and jurats, you will remember that the jurat requires the document signer to swear or affirm verbally to the notary that the statements within the signed document are true. An affidavit, which is sometimes referred to as a "statement of fact," is the written statement(s) within the document that the signer is representing as true.

The one signing the affidavit is often referred to as an "affiant." Since notarizing a document requiring a jurat also requires the oath or affirmation, a signer of a jurat is also called an affiant. As a notary, you may be presented with many forms that are either labeled as "affidavits" or by their nature are affidavits, and almost all of them will require a jurat.

**Q. There is no notary verbiage on the form. How do I notarize it?**

**A.** You will no doubt encounter many documents requiring notarization which either do not have any notary verbiage preprinted on them or have incorrect preprinted verbiage. In either case, you will need to know how to deal with this issue.

Our previous discussions have described in detail the proper wording for both acknowledgments and jurats, at least in California. If you are not a California notary, your state may have different requirements, but some states are not as particular regarding the exact verbiage used as California is. In any case, be sure to check the notary laws for your state.

Assuming there is no notary verbiage preprinted on the form, the notary must add the verbiage to the form either by hand, by stamp or by a separate page.

Few notaries will add the verbiage by hand, since the originators of a document do not like another person entering information by hand onto the document without their knowledge. If the document requires a jurat, the notary usually uses a jurat stamp, since it is rather small. However, if the requirement is for an acknowledgment, a separate acknowledgement form is filled out and attached to the document.

It is important to never use your notary seal on any document without notary verbiage. It is illegal, and you can have your commission suspended or revoked by the secretary of state.

As a notary, you should always carry acknowledgment forms, a jurat stamp and 2005 jurat forms, just in case you are required to notarize a document without the jurat verbiage in place or with the wrong jurat verbiage preprinted on it.

The following are examples of a blank acknowledgment form, a blank 2005 jurat form and a blank imprint of a jurat stamp.

**CALIFORNIA ALL-PURPOSE**
**CERTIFICATE OF ACKNOWLEDGMENT**

State of ______________ }
County of ______________ } ss.

On ______________ before me, ______________
(Date) (Notary)

personally appeared ______________
Signer(s)

personally known to me (or proved to me on the basis of satisfactory evidence) to be the person(s) whose name(s) is/are subscribed to the within instrument and acknowledged to me that he/she/they executed the same in his/her/their authorized capacity(ies), and that by his/her/their signature(s) on the instrument the person(s), or the entity upon behalf of which the person(s) acted, executed the instrument.

Stamp clear impression of notary seal above.

WITNESS my hand and official seal.

______________
Notary's Signature

OPTIONAL INFORMATION

**CAPACITY CLAIMED BY THE SIGNER**

- ☐ Individual (s)
- ☐ Corporate Officer

______________
(Title)

- ☐ Partner(s)
- ☐ Attorney-in-Fact
- ☐ Trustee(s)
- ☐ Other ______________

**DESCRIPTION OF THE ATTACHED**

______________
**Title of Document**

______________
**Number of Pages**

______________
**Document Date**

______________
**Other Information**

*California 2005 All-Purpose Acknowledgment.*
*Also called a "loose certificate."*

## Jurat

State of ______________ }
County of _____________ } ss.

Subscribed and sworn to (or affirmed) before me ____________________
Name of commissioned notary

on this ____________________ by ____________________
Date of notarization ... Name of affiant

☐ personally known to me or ☐ proved to me on the basis of satisfactory evidence

to be the person who appeared before me.

WITNESS my hand and official seal.

Stamp clear impression of notary seal above.

____________________
Notary's Signature

OPTIONAL INFORMATION

**DESCRIPTION OF THE ATTACHED**

____________________
**Title of Document**

____________________
**Number of Pages**

____________________
**Document Date**

____________________
**Other Information**

*California 2005 jurat, or "loose certificate."*

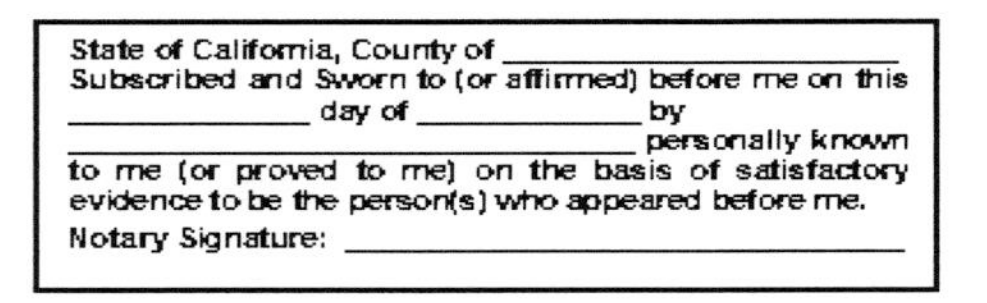
State of California, County of ____________________
Subscribed and Sworn to (or affirmed) before me on this
____________ day of ____________ by
____________________ personally known
to me (or proved to me) on the basis of satisfactory
evidence to be the person(s) who appeared before me.
Notary Signature: ____________________

*California jurat stamp after January 2005.*

**Q. I have to complete a jurat but I forgot the proper wording of the oath.**

**A.** There is no particular wording stipulated by California legislation regarding the exact form of the oath or affirmation a notary gives to an affiant. The California ***2005 Notary Public Handbook*** suggests the following:

"Do you swear or affirm that the statements in this document are true?"

Most notaries use either this statement or a variation. Two examples are:

> "Do you swear or affirm that all of the statements made in this document are true to the best of your knowledge, so help you God?"

> "Do you swear or affirm that all of the statements made in this document are true to the best of your knowledge?"

The only difference between the two previous questions is the reference to God. Some notaries prefer to use the reference and others prefer to omit it, out of deference to the affiant's possible beliefs.

Finally, while it is not required, most notaries request the affiant to raise his or her right hand while administering the oath or affirmation. The request is made primarily to remind the affiant of the seriousness of the statement, and to add a level of formality to the notarization process.

**Q. Do all jurats in California require proper identification?**

**A.** In California, all jurats completed after January 1, 2005, must include proper identification of the document signer(s). You will undoubtedly be presented with documents that have jurat statements preprinted and filled out that do not have the entire jurat verbiage for 2005. As stated in the previous sections, you must attach the correct verbiage before stamping the document with your notary seal, and you must verify the identity of the document signer. There are absolutely no exceptions made!

Subscribed and Sworn to before me

this ______________ day of __________, 19 ____________

_______________________________________________
Signature

Notary Public Commissioned for said County and State

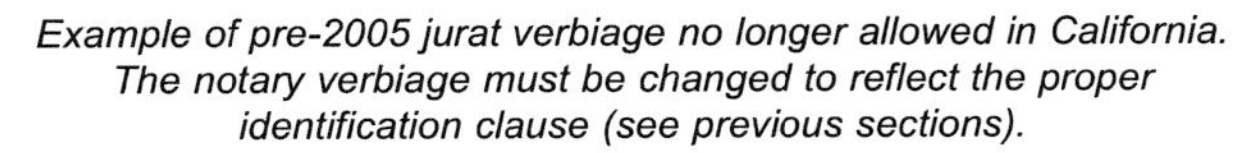

*Example of pre-2005 jurat verbiage no longer allowed in California. The notary verbiage must be changed to reflect the proper identification clause (see previous sections).*

**Q. Do all acknowledgments require proper identification?**

**A.** Acknowledgments always require proper identification of the document signer requesting notarization of his or her signature.

**Q. The document is clearly an affidavit, but the acknowledgment wording is preprinted for notarization. Should I attach a jurat anyway?**

**A.** In California, a non-attorney notary is not permitted to advise a client on which notary act to perform. If a client brings you a form that seems to have the wrong notarial verbiage printed, you are not permitted to advise the client otherwise.

It is possible that the document originators wished for the document signer to sign the affidavit statement, but were unconcerned with having the jurat process completed. Since prior to 2005 jurats did not include proving the identity of the document signer, the originators may have attached acknowledgment verbiage on the form to insure the proper identification of the signer.

As a notary, unless instructed otherwise by a client's attorney, you should complete the notary act requested of you. The request can be made either directly by the client or indirectly by whatever verbiage is indicated on the client's document. In this case, you should not attach a jurat to the form unless you have been requested to do so by the client, his or her attorney or the originator of the document.

**Q. What does "authorized capacities" mean in a California All-Purpose Acknowledgment?**

**A.** We have already discussed this in the first question of this chapter, "What is the difference between an acknowledgment and a jurat?" Of course, you may be skipping around to various questions so assuming that you have not yet read about authorized capacities, in California especially, notaries must know about this important area of notary law.

The state of California used to have different acknowledgment forms for the various capacities of document signers. For example, there were "Individual Acknowledgments" for persons who represented only themselves, "Corporate Acknowledgments" for signers representing a corporation, and so on. In the early 1990s, this was changed to an All-Purpose Acknowledgment form that allowed for any signer to claim an authorized capacity.

Consequently, now in California, an essential part of the acknowledgment process is that the document signer, with his or her signature is also acknowledging that he or she is signing in his or her authorized capacity. This means that if someone is signing as CEO of a company or a partner of a Limited Partnership, the signer does not need to prove that capacity to the notary. The very act of signing the document is enough to acknowledge to the notary that he or she is signing in an authorized capacity.

This is important because some states require the notary to verify the authorized capacity of a document signer, but not California. California notaries must be aware that since some states require the notary to verify the authorized capacity of the signer, acknowledgment wording for those states will be different from that in California.

The proper wording for an acknowledgment in California is:

State of ________________ }
County of ________________ } ss.

On ____________________ before me, ________________________
(Date) (Notary)

personally appeared ____________________________________
Signer(s)

personally known to me (or proved to me on the basis of satisfactory evidence) to be the person(s) whose name(s) is/are subscribed to the within instrument and acknowledged to me that he/she/they executed the same in his/her/their authorized capacity(ies), and that by his/her/their signature(s) on the instrument the person(s), or the entity upon behalf of which the person(s) acted, executed the instrument.

You should notice from this wording the signer is claiming his or her own authorized capacity.

Since some states require the notary to verify the authorized capacity of a signer, it is very possible that a document may be brought or sent to a notary in California which has been drawn in that state but is illegal for a California notary to notarize. For example:

STATE OF ____________

COUNTY OF ___________

On this _________ day of ______________, ___________, before me, the undersigned, a Notary Public in and for the State of ________________, duly commissioned and sworn personally appeared ________________________________ **to me known or proved to me** to be the ______________________ of ______________________, the corporation that executed the foregoing instrument and acknowledged the said instrument to be the free and voluntary act of and deed of said corporation, for the uses and purposes therein .

Notice the section requiring the notary to either know, or have proven to him or her, the signer's authorized capacity.

It is illegal for a notary in California to comply with a request from another state if it requires the notary to perform any action specifically prohibited by California notary legislation. Completing this acknowledgment is a perfect example of such an illegal request. Instead of filling out this acknowledgment wording, the notary in California must use a form called an All-Purpose Certificate of Acknowledgment containing the correct wording.

**Q. What does "WITNESS my hand and official seal" mean?**

**A.** Notary verbiage often includes this phrase that means the signature and seal in this section of the document is the official signature and seal of the notary public who actually performed the notarial services. You will want to place your seal as close to this wording as possible or the document might not be recorded.

**Q. What does "Subscribed and Sworn" mean?**

**A.** This verbiage, now on every jurat statement made in California, means the document signer signed the document in front of the notary and at the time of notarization. It also refers to the fact that the notary issued an oath or affirmation and the signer swore (or affirmed) to the veracity of the document.

Some notaries fail to physically issue the oath or affirmation. Failing to perform a jurat completely can result in a negation of the notary act, thereby subjecting the notary to serious consequences.

**Q. What does the SS. mean on many notary forms?**

**A.** Aside the venue on many notary forms you will find the denotation "SS." While they may make a legal document look official, their absence does not invalidate the form. "SS" is Latin for "scilicet" which means, "to wit," "that is to say" or "more particularly." So the venue state may be California, but more particularly, the county of Los Angeles.

**Q. What color ink should I use to fill out the acknowledgment or jurat?**

**A.** There is no legal requirement to use any particular color ink when completing these forms; however, most notaries always use either blue or black ink. The notary section must be photographically reproducible, and if you use a light color such as pink or green, either the document originator or the recorder may reject the document.

Sometimes, notaries are given instructions by the document originator concerning the required color (such as blue) for notarizing a particular document, but in most cases, the decision is up to the notary.

As important as it is to ensure that the notarization is photographically reproducible, it is equally important the information written by the notary be very legible. Most notaries print the information in the notary section for legibility, and of course, sign their name.

# ~ CHAPTER 5 ~
# Important Questions About Signers

**Q. How do I instruct the signer to sign the document?**

**A.** Every document presented before you for notarization will require the signature of the document signer. Sometimes, questions come up about how the document is to be signed.

The rule of thumb is that document signers should always sign the document exactly as their name appears within the document. So, if Jonathan S. Smith is named within the document, he should sign as Jonathan S. Smith. If he is named as Jonathan S. Smith II, he should sign accordingly.

Occasionally, a signer will object to signing his or her name exactly as it is appears within the document. In the above example, Jonathan S. Smith may tell you that he never signs with his middle initial, or he always signs legal documents as J.S. Smith. Explain to the signer that if the documents are not signed exactly as his or her name appears within them, they may not be considered properly executed and may not be recorded. Once a signer knows that the documents may not be considered properly executed if they are not signed correctly, very few will refuse.

Believe it or not, the document signer always retains the legal right to sign any way he or she wishes. You may notarize that signature but you may not write a name in the notary section of the document that has not been proven to you.

If a signer does refuse to sign the documents as instructed you may have to proceed with the signing.

If you have accepted the signing on behalf of a separate entity, politely excuse yourself for a minute and call whomever assigned you the job (title company, escrow company, lender, etc.). Inform the representative of the situation and give them an opportunity to speak with the signer first. If you cannot reach anyone, you will simply have to proceed.

Of course, the notary process requires you to complete the notary wording stating you have properly identified the person who signed the document. If Jonathan S. Smith is the name within the document and the signer refused to sign as Jonathan S. Smith but signed as J.S. Smith, whose name do you fill out in the notary section?

Suppose he used a driver's license for identification. Remember, in this case, Jonathan S. Smith is the name within the document but your signer demanded to sign the document with J.S. Smith. If the driver's license contains at least Jonathan S. Smith and he signed that license as J.S. Smith, than you have properly identified the person, Jonathan S. Smith.

The signature does not by itself identify a person. It is the identification document that identifies a person and the signature is a part of that identification document. Always use the name that appears throughout the document in your notary wording if possible.

If the name on the identification contains as much information as the name within the document being signed, and the signatures on both match, use the name listed on the document being signed in your notary wording.

**Q. The signer's signature is completely illegible. Should I have the signer print his or her name below the signature?**

**A.** Many people's signatures are illegible scribbles. Signers have the right to sign their name as they wish and if the signature is illegible, it is still their signature. As long as the signature matches the signature within the identification document, and that person has satisfactorily proven his or her identity to you, you may notarize the document.

However, in some cases, a recorder could reject a document if an illegible signature is not accompanied by the name typed or printed above or below the signature line, so many notaries ask signers with illegible signatures to print their names as they appear within the document (assuming the names in the document are correct) above or below their signatures.

If you are notarizing loan-signing documents, in almost every case, a signed document requiring recording will contain a typed signature line, or a place for the signer to print his or her name along with the signature.

**Q. The name on the document is misspelled. Should I correct the errors before signing?**

**A.** Sometimes the name within the document is misspelled or the middle initial is wrong. For example, Susan C. Smith may be incorrectly named as Susan O. Smith. You cannot allow the signer to sign his or name incorrectly, so if possible, you should obtain permission from the document originators to have the name corrected before proceeding. Most companies who originate documents do not want any changes made to them without authorization, even if there are obvious errors. Never make changes within the document without instruction.

Some companies prefer you to abandon the signing if the name is misspelled within the document, but most will want you to notarize the document, therefore saving the signing. If you are notarizing loan documents and accept an assignment for a company you have never worked with, you should always try to find out their preferences for such circumstances before you proceed. Many companies have written documentation which can be faxed to you outlining their policies. As long as these policies do not require you to do something illegal, follow them closely.

Call whomever assigned the job and request authorization for the signer to reprint his or her name correctly within the document. If the change is allowed, the signer will also be required to initial each modification. If permission is not granted or you cannot reach anyone, assuming that the signer does not object, the signer may elect to sign the document correctly.

You must verify that the signature matches the one on the identification document, and you must always write the correct name as proven to you in the notary verbiage, even if it has been misspelled throughout the document.

In this case, since Susan C. Smith is the correct spelling of her name, and that spelling is verified by her identification document, you must indicate that it was Susan C. Smith who personally appeared and proved her identity to you on the notary section.

If the signer's name was previously typed for you in the notary wording and that name is spelled incorrectly, you must cross off the incorrect spelling and write the name correctly. ***The notary wording is the only text within loan-signing documents you may change without permission from the document originators.***

Loan-signing documents will need to be sent back to your client after the signing is completed, so always include a separate note with them informing the client the name was misspelled throughout the document. Indicate that attempts at reaching the originators were unsuccessful, but the signer signed the documents with his or her correct spelling.

Loan-signing documents usually have a "Limited Correction Agreement" included, which allows the originators of the document to correct any typos or clerical errors within it. This agreement will usually be sufficient for the correction of a misspelled name. If not, as a loan signer, your choice was to abandon the loan signing or to legally comply with the wishes of the signer, and perhaps save the signing. The worst-case scenario is that the signing will have to be repeated, but if you had abandoned the signing you would have had to repeat it anyway.

Remember that the signer always retains the right to sign the document, even if the signature is different from the name within the document. As long as you properly identify the signer, and your notary wording reflects the name of the person who proved his or her identity to you, you have legally complied with notary law. Most companies will appreciate your professionalism.

**Q. The name in the document does not match the name on the identification. Which name do I use?**

**A.** This common problem causes headaches for many notaries. Dealing with it correctly is essential to not only saving a signing, but keeping yourself out of trouble. Read this section carefully because it can be a bit difficult to conceptualize.

The rule of thumb is that document signers should always sign the document exactly as their name appears within it. That name should also match the identification, such as a driver's license or passport. If Jonathan S. Smith is named within the document, he should sign as Jonathan S. Smith and his driver's license should reflect at least Jonathan S. Smith. Whenever possible, stick to that rule.

In reality, things can get much more complicated. Quite often people use abbreviations, nicknames, hyphenated or multiple surnames. Sometimes, people change their names, or use one name when signing legal documents and another name for everything else.

Make it a ritual to always check the driver's license, passport or other form of identification before the client signs the document. If there are problems, you will catch them before the client signs. ***Remember, if you are using an identification document such as a driver's license, to verify identity, it can contain more information than the name within the document or signature, but never less.***

For example, a driver's license with the name, Jonathan S. Smith may be used for someone signing the document as Jonathan S. Smith, Jonathan Smith, and even J. S. Smith, but not for Jonathan Samuel Smith (the license does not have Samuel), or Jonathan S. Smith Jr. (the license does not have Jr.). Nor can it be used if there is a different spelling of the name. For example, for purposes of proving identification, John Smith is not necessarily the same person as Jonathan Smith, and if the driver's license has John Smith, it cannot be used to verify identity for Jonathan Smith.

Another problem occurs with nicknames or abbreviated names. Betty is often a nickname for Elizabeth and Dick is often a nickname for Richard. As a notary, you cannot assume that Betty and Elizabeth are the same person unless you have additional verified evidence.

Even though Tom is usually an abbreviated version of Thomas, it is not necessarily so. Similarly, Junior can be a nickname for John Jones Jr. but not necessarily.

Let me reiterate that the name on the identification (a driver's license, for example) does not have to exactly match the name on the document being notarized nor the signature. The name on the identification document can contain more information than the name within the document or signature, but never less.

As long as the identification contains the same information or more information than the name on the document and signature, it can be used for identification. If Liz Brown is on the document to be notarized and Elizabeth Brown is on her driver's license, the license can be used because "Liz" appears in both.

So, what do you do when the name on the document and signature do not match the name on the identification, and there are no alternatively acceptable identification documents. How can you proceed?

First, in California, you can always use credible witnesses if they are available. If you are a notary in another state, check your state's credible-witness laws. If you are unfamiliar with using credible witnesses, please review Chapter 16 in this book. Most of the time, credible witnesses can be found by asking the document signer to call neighbors or relatives who do not have a beneficial or financial interest in the document. If credible witnesses cannot be found, you have only two options left or you will need to abandon the signing and reschedule.

Since the document signer retains the legal right to sign the document any way he or she wishes, the signer might demand to sign a name that is different than the name in the document. Notarize that signature, but complete the notarization with the name as signed. I should point out that since entering a different name on the acknowledgment than indicated in the document would probably cause that document to be rejected, the document originator might blame you for a faulty notarization, even though it is correct. The documents will probably have to be redrawn, re-signed and re-notarized, and everyone could be unhappy.

Unfortunately, once you make the client aware of the problem with identification and he or she chooses to ignore your concerns, since the law says you may not provide legal advice, if his or her identification documents match the signature and physical description (picture), you must notarize the signature.

Be careful on this point. If the document signer demands to use something in his or her signature that does not match the identification, such as "Jr.," you simply must decline the notarization unless another form of identification with the "Jr." can be presented.

You do have another option. You can ask the signer to call the document originator or lender to inform them of the issue and ask if it is acceptable to change the name by hand everywhere in the document so it matches the name on the identification. Most of the time the lender or document originator will say "no," and will instruct the signer to sign his or her name exactly as it appears, regardless of what name is on the driver's license.

In most cases there is a document included with a loan package that lists variations of the document-signer's name. This document may have one of several titles, but it is commonly referred to as a "Signature Name Affidavit." It states that the signer swears that he or she is the same person as all of the name variations listed. For example, a name affidavit for Daniel C. Jones may read:

- Daniel Jones
- Daniel C. Jones
- Daniel C. Jones Jr.
- Dan Jones
- D.C. Jones

The lender will usually point to this document as proof that Daniel C. Jones Jr. (as named within the document) is the same person as Daniel C. Jones (as named on the identification). This Signature Name Affidavit may be acceptable proof for the lender, but cannot be used as proof of identity for the notary.

This is my personal suggestion on this subject. Never subject yourself to the possibility of fraud just to save a client some trouble or to save a signing. The best way to handle such a situation is to anticipate the problem. If you notarize a lot of documents, you will unquestionably be faced sooner or later with this kind of issue, and will need to become comfortable with how to handle it when it comes up.

Prevent the problem in the first place. When a lender or escrow company calls you for a loan signing, find out their policies for these kinds of problems first. Be sure to call the document signer before you go to the signing. Find out if he or she has proper identification by asking the signer to read the name as it is printed on the identification document he or she will be using. Compare it with the name on the documents to be signed, since you will have these in hand before you go to the signing. Be sure to check expiration dates as well.

If you see a problem, ask if the signer has an alternative source for proving identity. Can credible witnesses be available when you arrive? You do not want to wait an hour or more inside the signer's home or office while credible witnesses are being rounded up. If no credible witnesses are available, notify the lender or whomever called you immediately.

Describe the problem in detail and explain why you cannot use the identification documents. Perhaps the documents can be redrawn and sent to you before the signing.

If you are working from an office and someone comes in spontaneously to notarize a document and you cannot verify his or her identity properly, you will simply have to decline the notarization. Suggest that the documents be redrawn or the signer find a notary who personally knows him or her.

I have one final point for clarification on this topic. You already know that you cannot include name information in the notary verbiage which has not been proven to you. Similarly, you should not include additional name information in the notary verbiage that is not required to be there just because it is listed on the identification document.

Once again, as long as the identification contains the same or more information as the name within the document being notarized, the signatures on both match, and the physical description including the photograph are reasonably close, you have properly identified the signer. In your notary verbiage write the name exactly as it is spelled within the document, regardless of what is on the identification.

If, as in our previous example, Jonathan S. Smith is named in the document and signs the document and his signature matches his identification, which states that he is Jonathan Samuel Smith, and if you are completing an acknowledgment, you will write "personally appeared ***Jonathan S. Smith***" not "***Jonathan Samuel Smith***," since even though that name appears on his driver's license, it is more information than required on the document to be notarized.

You may wonder, why this would be a problem? After all, would it not be better to have more information in the notary verbiage than just exactly what is needed? The answer is no. If the documents are being drawn for Jonathan S. Smith and you put in the notary verbiage Jonathan Samuel Smith, the documents will be very likely be rejected. Always match what is in the document exactly unless it is impossible. Then, follow the guidelines presented in this section.

Finally, we need to deal with multiple or hyphenated last names and first names which are meant to reflect a title or religious affiliation. Many cultures throughout the world have established a tradition of using both maternal and paternal surnames. If Carmen O'Brien-Smith is on the document but the identification only has Carmen O'Brien or Carmen Smith, you cannot use the identification since it has less information than required. If, however, the document lists Carmen Smith as the signer and the identification has Carmen O'Brien-Smith, you may use the identification.

If the name on a document is Mohammed Amed Sukar but the identification document omits Mohammed, you must find an alternative source of identification. Even though the signer may protest by suggesting that the first name Mohammed is more of a cultural or religious title than a name, the document originators are treating it as a legal first name and you must as well.

**Q. The notary verbiage has already been typed out for two signers but only one signer is present. Can I change the verbiage by hand?**

**A.** Let's look at the following example of a grant deed requiring two signatures:

GRANT DEED
Joint Tenancy

FOR VALUABLE CONSIDERATION, receipt of which is acknowledged, I (we) Robert Smith and Mary Smith, husband and wife
(NAME OF GRANTOR(S))

grant to Peter Jones and Janet Jones, husband and wife,
(NAME OF GRANTEE(S))

, AS JOINT TENANTS,
all that real property situated in the City of Orange (or in an unincorporated area of) Orange County, State of Ca, described as follows (insert legal description):
Lot 11, of Tract number 16467, as recorded in Book 24, pages 12-13 of the Orange County recorder

Assessor's Parcel No: 00922000
Executed on August 21, 2005 at Anaheim, CA
(CITY AND STATE)

STATE OF CA
COUNTY OF Orange
On August 21, 2005 before me, ____________
(Name/Title, i.e. "Jane Doe, Notary Public")

personally appeared Robert Smith and Mary Smith personally known to me (or proved to me on the basis of satisfactory evidence) to be the person(s) whose name(s) is/are subscribed to the within instrument and acknowledged to me that he/she/they executed the same in his/her/their authorized capacity(ies), and that by his/her/their signature(s) on the instrument the person(s), or the entity upon behalf of which the person(s) acted, executed the instrument.

WITNESS my hand and official seal.

(SIGNATURE OF NOTARY) (SEAL)

This document requiring the signatures of Robert Smith and Mary Smith has already been filled out, and the notary wording already completed by the originator. This is sometimes done to eliminate a possible error if the notary were to write the name in this section.

The lender assumes that both parties will sign the document in front of the notary at the same time, but this is not always possible. Suppose Mary Smith is unavailable on the day and time that Robert Smith takes the document to a notary?

Suppose only Robert Smith appears before the notary on that day and time. The notary must cross off Mary Smith's name and complete the notarization for Robert Smith only. It is imperative that the notary follows the required guidelines of indicating the correct singular/plural word choices as well as the correct pronouns in the subsequent notary verbiage.

Robert Smith

STATE OF CA

COUNTY OF Orange

On August 21, 2005 before me, Daniel C. Jones, Notary Public

personally appeared Robert Smith ~~and Mary Smith~~ ~~personally known to me~~ (or proved to me on the basis of satisfactory evidence) to be the person~~(s)~~ whose name~~(s)~~ is~~/are~~ subscribed to the within instrument and acknowledged to me that he~~/she/they~~ executed the same in his~~/her/their~~ authorized capacity~~(ies)~~, and that by his~~/her/their~~ signature~~(s)~~ on the instrument the person~~(s)~~, or the entity upon behalf of which the person~~(s)~~ acted, executed the instrument.

WITNESS my hand and official seal.

Daniel C. Jones
(SIGNATURE OF NOTARY) (SEAL)

**Q. The document has already been signed. Does the signer have to sign again in front of me?**

**A.** This depends on the notary act required. Acknowledgments do not require that the document signer actually sign the document in front of the notary, only that he or she acknowledges his or her signature.

If a document requiring an acknowledgment has already been signed, the notary simply asks the signer a question such as, "Is this signature yours?" The signer should say "yes" and you can move on. He or she has acknowledged his or her signature before you.

On the other hand, if a document requires a jurat, jurat verbiage indicates the words "Subscribed and Sworn (or affirmed) before me," and consequently does require that the document signer sign in front of the notary.

If the document has already been signed and requires a jurat, the notary must administer the oath or affirmation and must require that the signer re-sign the document at that time.

**Q. One of the signers does not speak English. Can I still notarize the signature if I do not speak his or her language?**

**A.** Notary law prohibits notaries from notarizing the signature of someone if they are unable to communicate with that person in a common language. If you are called upon to notarize a document for a couple who speak only Korean, and you do not speak any Korean, you are not permitted to complete the notary act. The clients are supposed to find another notary who speaks their language. Of course, this law often becomes quite impractical. With more than 6,000 spoken languages in the world, finding a notary who speaks a language other than English or Spanish is usually difficult. The most commonly spoken language in the world is Mandarin Chinese, yet finding a Mandarin-speaking notary in the United States is very difficult, time-consuming and often impossible to do, given that most documents are time-sensitive.

Why not use an interpreter? That also is illegal according to notary law. Most notaries who arrive at a signing to find out communication is impossible with one or more of the parties end up using a friend or relative of the signer and complete the signing anyway. Notarizing documents for a signer with whom you cannot communicate can put you at risk for a serious lawsuit and prosecution.

The only good news is that neither of you have to be fluent speakers of a common language; just enough to communicate. If, for example, your client is a Spanish-speaker and you can speak enough Spanish that you are satisfied in meeting the requirement of being able to communicate (and would be willing and able to prove your level of knowledge of Spanish in court, if required), then complete the notarization. If the client can speak a level of English sufficient enough to adequately communicate with you, then you are permitted to notarize. We all have spoken with persons whose first language is not English and even though their English is rough, they are still communicating and we have understood what they have said.

When you accept an assignment from a client such as an escrow company and you suspect that because the surname is foreign the client may not speak English, consider asking your client to verify that the signer indeed can communicate in English before accepting the assignment.

**Q. There is more than one document signer but only one acknowledgment. What should I do?**

**A.** A single acknowledgment may be used for more than one document signer, as long as each document signer named within the acknowledgment is present at the same time for notarization. You already know the verbiage in the acknowledgment indicates singular and plural forms for signers, which the notary must notate during the notary process. For example, notice the acknowledgment verbiage has the options "his/her/their" or "capacity(ies)" for which the notary is to either circle the correct form or cross out the incorrect forms.

The important thing to remember when completing a single acknowledgment for more than one person is that all persons named on that acknowledgment must appear at the same time. If they appear at different times, you must use separate acknowledgments. This is because when you are completing a notary act, you must fully complete the notary act at that time. You must place your notary seal on the document or acknowledgment form, and enter the information about that notary act, including the date and time, in your notary journal.

If two or more document signers appear at different times for notarization, simply complete a separate acknowledgment form for each person at the time of notarization. You should always have extra acknowledgment forms with you. If you need additional forms, www.notaryclasses.com has a CD called "Essential Notary Forms." It contains acknowledgments and many other forms that you can print out whenever you need them.

**Q. There is more than one document signer but only one jurat. What should I do?**

**A.** A single jurat may be used for multiple signers but you will probably not be able to fit more than a single person's name in the space allotted if you are using a jurat stamp. Simply use your jurat stamp for the additional signers or attach jurat forms. Keep in mind that the verbiage for California jurats changed in 2005 and you must use the 2005 verbiage.

As with acknowledgments, you should always have extra jurat forms with you. If you need additional forms, www.notaryclasses.com has a CD called "Essential Notary Forms" with jurat forms and many others you can print out whenever you need them.

**Q. The document requires that both the husband and wife sign. and each of their signatures be notarized. Only the husband is present. What should I do?**

**A.** You may only notarize the document for the person or persons who appear before you at the time of notarization, so in this case, you would notarize the husband's signature only. Keep in mind that you will have to use a separate acknowledgment when the wife comes to have her signature notarized later. If the document already has both the husband's and wife's name pre-typed in the acknowledgment section, simply cross out the name of the person who is not appearing before you at that moment. Remember to complete the proper pronouns and plural/singular forms for the rest of the notary verbiage.

Robert Smith

STATE OF CA

COUNTY OF Orange

On August 21, 2005 before me, Daniel C. Jones, Notary Public
[illegible]

personally appeared Robert Smith ~~and Mary Smith~~ ~~personally known to me~~ (or proved to me on the basis of satisfactory evidence) to be the person~~(s)~~ whose name~~(s)~~ is~~/are~~ subscribed to the within instrument and acknowledged to me that he~~/she/they~~ executed the same in his~~/her/their~~ authorized capacity~~(ies)~~, and that by his~~/her/their~~ signature~~(s)~~ on the instrument the person~~(s)~~, or the entity upon behalf of which the person~~(s)~~ acted, executed the instrument.

WITNESS my hand and official seal.

Daniel C. Jones
(SIGNATURE OF NOTARY) (SEAL)

# ~ CHAPTER 6 ~
# Proper Notary Procedures

**Q. Should I make copies of everything I notarize?**

**A.** It is not necessary to make copies of the documents you notarize. Some states do, however, require that you make copies of any documents you certify. Check with your own state requirements if you are certifying a document.

**Q. Do I have to read through the entire document before I can notarize it?**

**A.** It is not the responsibility of the notary to read the document before notarizing it, but the notary does have to look through the document for blank spaces or incomplete areas. It is against the law to notarize a blank or incomplete document. You would not know if the document is complete without reviewing it first.

**Q. Someone has brought me the last page of a multi-page document to notarize. Do I have to request all of the other pages first?**

**A.** Quite often a client will present just the signature page of a document to you and request you notarize his or her signature without seeing the rest of the document. You must ask the client to present the rest of the document in its entirety. It must be completely filled out prior to notarization.

**Q. There are a lot of blank spaces in the document. What should I do?**

**A.** In going through the document, if you notice blank or incomplete spaces, you will need to halt the notary process until this is cleared up. If you are at a loan signing you may need to contact the lender or escrow company. Otherwise, tell your client that you are not permitted to notarize the document and leave the decision about what to do to him or her.

Of course, some areas are intentionally left blank because they are not applicable. The important idea here is to help someone avoid signing a document and then having information added to it later, in a blank area, that the client would not have agreed with at all.

For example, suppose the lien amount was left blank in a deed of trust. An unscrupulous lender may enter a lien amount later that was not originally agreed to by the signer. Of course, a legal battle may ensue, but a portion of your notary process is to examine the forms for these important blank or incomplete spaces to help avoid legal battles.

**Q. The document signer has no idea how to fill out the form to be notarized. How can I help him or her?**

**A.** Unless you are also an attorney, you must refrain from assisting your clients in filling out forms. If you help the client with his or her forms and the client later has legal repercussions, there may be an action against you for illegally providing legal services.

A great example of this would be in property-transfer documents, such as a grant deed. There are many ways to take title to property, commonly known as "vesting." For example, a husband and wife may choose to vest title as "Joint Tenants" or "Community Property with Rights of Survivorship," or even as "Tenants in Common." Each vesting has serious tax implications, especially upon the death of one or both spouses. As a notary, suggesting a particular vesting for your client can lead to trouble for you later if one member of the couple decides to sue you. Helping a client to fill out the transfer document will only provide additional evidence of your assistance.

In California, there is an exception to this rule: if you are an immigration consultant as recognized by the state, you may assist your client in completing his or her immigration documents. Keep in mind that California has placed a limit on the fees you may charge for this service.

**Q. I really have no idea what this document means. Can I still notarize it?**

**A.** As a notary, you are not responsible for the content of the document to be notarized and consequently, it is irrelevant whether or not you understand it. You are simply notarizing the signature of your client, not guaranteeing the veracity of the document.

Remember that you should look over the document in its entirety to ensure that it is complete. Notary legislation requires the document to be complete before notarizing. Of course, you cannot always determine whether the document is complete or not, so the law has been written in such a manner that you should be able to determine whether the document is "on its face" or obviously incomplete or not. This provision really helps the notary should some blank space appear buried within the document that is not obvious.

That said, you should become familiar with documents that you will notarize on a consistent basis. For example, suppose you notarize grant deeds frequently, and a client brings you a grant deed to be notarized without a grantee listed or a legal description noted. Of course the recorder's office will not accept the document until completed, but unintended information can be added to these areas, especially after notarization. Becoming familiar with these documents will help you avoid fraud and keep you out of trouble.

**Q. Someone has a document written in Chinese and I cannot read it. What should I do?**

**A.** Contrary to popular belief, you are indeed permitted to notarize a document in a language that you cannot read. It will still be necessary to peruse the document for obviously blank or incomplete spaces. Of course, this begs the question of, "If I cannot read the document, how can I know if there is missing information which is vital to it?" The key here is whether something is obviously missing or "on its face" is blank or incomplete.

When a notary completes the notary act, they have guaranteed certain things about the signer:

1. He or she personally appeared before the notary at the time of notarization;
2. He or she either signed the document in the presence of the notary or acknowledged to the notary that the signature on the document is indeed his or her signature;
3. The document signer was properly identified;
4. If required, the signer took an oath regarding the truthfulness of the document;
5. If the signature is being acknowledged, the signer is signing the document in an authorized capacity.

The notary is not guaranteeing anything else about this document, other than the document did not have obvious blank or incomplete spaces at the time of notarization.

Remember you must be able to communicate with the document signer in a common language or you must decline to complete the notary act.

Suppose for example, you had been called upon to notarize a prenuptial agreement drawn up by the man but to be signed by both parties. Suppose the document is in Japanese or Korean or any other language which is common to both parties, but one which you do not speak at all.

Furthermore, the man speaks enough English to communicate with you but the woman speaks absolutely no English whatsoever. You presume, of course, that the woman understands the document since it is written in her language, but you cannot communicate with her except perhaps through the man who speaks both languages.

While you may certainly notarize his signature, you may not notarize her signature, because you cannot communicate directly with her. You are not even permitted to use an interpreter.

**Q. A friend has requested that I notarize a document he signed and wishes to fax it over to me, since he is unable to be present before me during notarization. Since he is a good friend, I don't mind. Will that be OK?**

**A.** The quickest way to lose your commission as well as face possible criminal charges is to notarize a document for someone who does not personally appear before you at the time of notarization. Every notary has a friend who wants a favor every now and then and the most common request is to notarize a signature on a document without the friend having to appear personally.

Both the acknowledgment and the jurat indicate a date of notarization that also specifically states that the signer personally appeared before the notary. Notarizing this document without the person's personal appearance can subject you to serious consequences.

A new law in California, effective January 2006 considers falsifying an acknowledgment forgery. Forgery is a felony and besides possible criminal conviction, obviously results in automatic revocation of your commission.

Friends of notaries will want favors every now and then, but this is one favor you absolutely must decline.

**Q. A California document already has an acknowledgment preprinted below, but the wording does not include the term "authorized capacities." What should I do?**

**A.** In the early 1990s, California acknowledgments changed from multiple acknowledgment forms reflecting the various capacities of signers to an "All-Purpose" acknowledgment format. There used to be separate acknowledgment forms, such as "Individual Acknowledgments," Corporate Acknowledgments," and so on, depending on the capacity of the document signer.

Fortunately, California has done away with all of these different acknowledgment forms by using the term "authorized capacities," and calling the form an "All-Purpose Acknowledgment."

Unfortunately, not everyone in California knows about this change, so as a notary, you may still see a document with outdated acknowledgment verbiage omitting the term "authorized capacities."

If a document is to be recorded in California, whether drawn up in California or another state, the acknowledgment verbiage must be exactly as indicated in previous chapters. If it is not present in its exact form, you must add the verbiage by using an All-Purpose Acknowledgment form, also known as a "loose certificate." If you notarize a document by acknowledgment which is to be recorded in California but does not have this verbiage exactly, the county recorder will reject the document and will require re-notarization. This can cause a significant time loss for your client and could cause more serious problems such as a delay in a loan closing. You must be aware of this law if you are a notary in California, as it will certainly affect you.

There are a large number of documents still out there, even in California, which have not incorporated the correct verbiage. If a document is not being recorded in California you have greater discretion. You may use the preprinted acknowledgment format as long as the acknowledgment does not require you as the notary to personally verify the authorized capacity of the signer. If, however, the document has no acknowledgment verbiage and the client wishes an acknowledgment to be performed, if you are notarizing in California, you must use the full acknowledgment verbiage as printed in the previous chapter, which includes the "authorized capacities" clause.

Keep in mind other states do not necessarily require the term "authorized capacities" with their acknowledgments. If a document is to be recorded outside of California and has preprinted acknowledgment verbiage which omits the "authorized capacity" verbiage, you may use that state's acknowledgment verbiage. By the way, you are not expected to know the notary laws of other states, so if the document you have been presented with is incorrect for that state, you are not expected to know that. If it is incorrect, the county recorder in that state may require that the document be re-notarized, but you will not be held responsible.

New notaries sometimes feel a bit overwhelmed with this requirement for California and consequently choose to use a California All-Purpose Acknowledgment form for every document requiring an acknowledgment, regardless of the state in which the document will be recorded. While this may seem to cover all the bases, realize that if you are notarizing documents for a client which will be recorded in a state other than California, those documents may have the verbiage just as that state wants it.

Most clients do not want you to add additional documents such as a California All-Purpose Acknowledgment form, and it is not necessary. As long as the document is to be recorded outside of California, you may use the verbiage preprinted on the acknowledgment section as long as that verbiage does not require you to do anything which is illegal for California notaries. Once again, however, if there is no verbiage provided, and the client requests an acknowledgment, California notaries are obligated to use the proper All-Purpose Acknowledgment form.

If you need to order California All-Purpose Acknowledgments, go to www.notaryclassses.com and purchase the CD of "Essential Notary Forms." The price is very reasonable and you will have just about any form you will need as a notary on one CD.

**Q. A California document already has jurat wording preprinted at the bottom, but the wording does not include anything about identification of the signer. Can I still use this form?**

**A.** California has had numerous changes to notary legislation, and one of the most recent at the time of this printing is the requirement for notaries to properly identify document signers for jurats. This procedure includes a substantial change to jurat verbiage which now incorporates the law requiring identity verification. Prior to this law taking effect in 2005, jurat acts did not require proof of identification for the document signer.

While almost every notary required proof of identity as a matter of formality, if a signer did not have proper identification and requested a jurat, the notary was required to complete the jurat without the proof of identification.

Consequently, there are a great many documents in California with preprinted jurat verbiage that does not incorporate the new clause for identification. Below, is a properly-worded jurat.

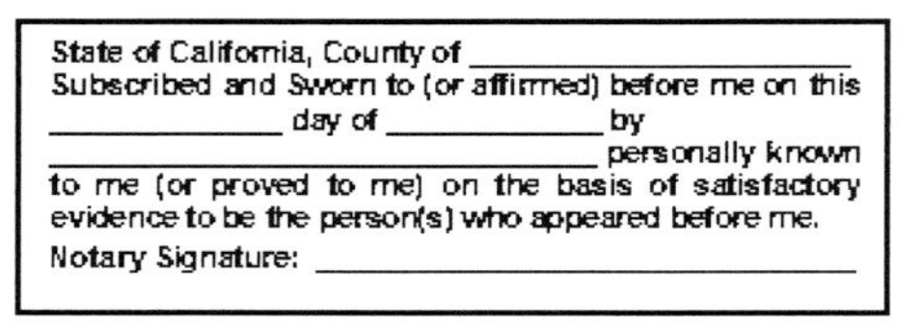
State of California, County of ____________________
Subscribed and Sworn to (or affirmed) before me on this
____________ day of ___________ by
_____________________________ personally known
to me (or proved to me) on the basis of satisfactory evidence to be the person(s) who appeared before me.
Notary Signature: ____________________________

*Example of a properly-worded jurat for California incorporating 2005 legislation requiring notaries to identify the document signer.*

If you are notarizing documents in California and the document requires a jurat, regardless of where the document will ultimately be recorded or even if it will be recorded, you must use proper California notary verbiage for jurats. The notary now is obligated to properly identify the document signer of a jurat ... no exceptions!

Since most documents still do not have the proper verbiage preprinted on them, you will need to purchase either a new, correct jurat stamp or use a new jurat form. The latter is available on the CD "Essential Notary Forms" offered by www.notaryclasses.com. If you do not have the proper forms or the proper jurat stamp, you will need to write the phrase as noted above in the example by hand.

**Q. My boss is asking me to notarize documents that he signed a few days ago. What should I tell him?**

**A.** Many notaries perform most of their notarial duties as a part of their employment responsibilities. It is critical that notaries who perform notary acts understand the laws that govern their actions, as quite often an employer may ask the notary to do something that is actually illegal. It is not necessarily an intentional request for you to do something illegal, but employers are not always familiar with proper notary procedure. An example of this might be when an employer signs a document and puts it into your inbox with a note to notarize it.

Of course, as long as the employer is present and you have personal access to him or her, notarizing the document would require you to meet with the employer personally at the time you complete the notarization, regardless of whether the document was previously signed. If the employer is not present when you are ready to notarize, you must wait until he or she returns and can be present before you.

Let's look at a typical scenario that may occur in any office environment. Suppose your employer signed some documents requiring notarization several days ago just prior to leaving on a business trip. Perhaps you were on vacation that particular day and he or she left instructions to notarize it upon your return and then fax it to the meeting he or she would be attending.

You have a bit of a problem here, as notary law specifically prohibits you from notarizing a document for someone who does not personally appear before you at the time of notarization. A subscribing witness may be used in this case, but you are not permitted to notarize that document, with either an acknowledgment or a jurat, since the signer is not present in front of you at the time of notarization.

Furthermore, new laws in California now make it a felony forgery if you falsify any information on an acknowledgment form, including the date of personal appearance. If you are caught in this situation, you may want to review the section on how to use a subscribing witness or "Proof of Execution" in Chapter 19.

The bottom line is this: never perform a notary act for anyone for any reason unless you are face-to-face with that person or you are completing a Proof of Execution. Even in the latter exception of a Proof of Execution, you still need to be face-to-face with the subscribing witness. You are actually notarizing his or her signature as subscribing witness, and not the signature of your employer as we find in this example.

**Q. I sign my name so many times a day I would prefer to use a signature stamp. Is this legal?**

**A.** Using a signature stamp for notary work is both illegal and foolish. Notary law is specific in that the notary must sign the official notary paperwork at the time of notarization. There is not much more to add about this. Someone stealing both your notary seal and your signature stamp, if you have one, could cause enormous difficulties for both you and those who fall victim to the thief's illegal notarizations.

There are already enough means of fraud for unscrupulous individuals and adding an invitation such as a signature stamp seems unwise.

**Q. I have forgotten my thumbprint pad. What can I do?**

**A.** Certain types of documents absolutely require a thumbprint. Property-transfer documents such as deeds of trust, grant deeds, quitclaim deeds, and warranty deeds require a thumbprint in the notary's official journal. What happens if you forget your thumbprint pad and you find yourself notarizing one of these documents requiring a thumbprint?

You cannot legally complete the notary process without obtaining a thumbprint in your journal. If you cannot come up with an innovative method of obtaining the print, you will need to reschedule the notary signing. This creates an enormous inconvenience for all involved, so you might try to come up with something which will save the signing.

For example, perhaps the client has a stamp pad you could use or perhaps you could quickly run out to the nearest drugstore and purchase one. Finding thumbprint pads might not be easy, but in a pinch, a cheap stamp pad will do. The ink simply needs to be permanent in your journal.

**Q. A co-worker has asked me to notarize a letter to an insurance company which I know she has falsified, but have no way of proving it. Am I required to notarize the letter anyway?**

**A.** A notary has a legal obligation to decline any notary act on any document that he or she knows contains falsified information. If a notary does perform a notary act on a document for which he or she knows contains false information, the notary may be guilty of a misdemeanor and the notary commission will be revoked. Additionally, anyone knowingly requesting a notary to notarize a document that contains falsified information could face criminal prosecution.

**Q. Can I notarize a document that has been faxed or e-mailed to me?**

**A.** There is no problem with notarizing faxed or e-mailed documents so long as the document signer is personally appearing before you at the time of notarization. Some notaries believe that the notarization can only be completed on original documents, but this is not the case. It is absolutely imperative however, that a notary does not notarize a faxed or e-mailed document for someone not appearing before the notary at the time of notarization.

**Q. An attorney has called me to request a copy of one of my journal entries. Should I just photocopy and fax those over?**

**A.** Any member of the public can request a copy of a journal record by written request, but the request must include the following information:

1. The name of the document signer.
2. The type of notary act performed.
3. The month and year in which the notary act was performed.

If an attorney or any other member of the public requests a specific journal record entry, you will need to cover the other records on the page when you copy that particular item so the other records are not also copied. You may then forward this copy to the requesting party preferably by certified mail, although there is no law prohibiting sending via fax or e-mail.

**Q. Do I have to notarize a document for someone who is belligerent and rude to me?**

**A.** Notary legislation requires a notary to notarize any document properly presented to the notary, as long as the requester can provide proper identification and pay for the services. Yet, we all know that there are people out there who can be obnoxious and even dangerous.

We as notaries are public servants performing important services on behalf of the state for clients from all walks of life. As public servants, we need to demonstrate patience and consideration for everyone that we can; however, if you are facing someone so rude and obnoxious that you actually fear for your own safety, leave the signing immediately.

Use as much diplomacy as possible in order to avoid confrontation, but you are under no obligation to remain in an environment so hostile that you are concerned for your own safety or the safety of others.

Be sure to record the reason for abandoning the notarization in your journal so if the person does complain to the secretary of state, you will be able to quickly recall just why you chose to leave.

In reality, the vast majority of notary assignments are good experiences. Remember that even though loan signers enter into the homes of strangers, there is a lot of documentation on those persons well before a notary is even called. As with any other type of work, some danger may exist, so you need to always remain cautious and alert. If a client becomes upset after reading the loan documents because of something unexpected in the documents, such as a higher interest rate than expected, remind the person that you are the notary and your function is completely separate from the lending company. You can remind the signer of the three-day right of rescission if applicable. You can suggest that he or she call the loan officer or representative for further clarification.

In very rare instances a situation may escalate to the point where a notary feels threatened; be aware that this possibility exists. If you are concerned about someone who is agitated and refuses to calm down, leave immediately and suggest that the client speak with his or her loan representative at the earliest convenience. As in every arena in life, stay aware and exercise diplomacy, courtesy and control over your situation.

If you feel any loss of control over your environment that you believe could lead to your endangerment, leave before the situation worsens. My suggestion is to use diplomacy whenever possible but protect yourself first; explain your actions later if required.

**Q. I notarized a set of loan documents two days ago, and the lender is calling me requesting that I notarize another document to be included in that package. He or she states that the acknowledgment must reflect the same date as the rest of the package. What should I do?**

**A.** Any notary who has worked as a loan signer for any significant length of time has received a call like this. Usually the lender will suggest that the notary simply forgot to notarize one of the documents, which may or may not be the case, but once in a while a document is to be added to the package that was not included with the original loan-signing documents.

A notary is in the proverbial Catch-22 with this situation. It is illegal to comply with the request to backdate an acknowledgment; but if the notary does not backdate, the notary's valued client could be quite upset and the notary risks the business relationship. The fact is that ***it is illegal to backdate an acknowledgment for any reason.*** The notary act must be completed at the time of notarization, which also means that the acknowledgment forms are to be completed, signed and stamped at the time of notarization.

The right way to handle this problem is to go back to the document signer and complete the acknowledgment legally. Of course, as real life would have it, what is right is not always convenient and sometimes downright very difficult. Suppose a loan must close on a specific date or the buyer loses his or her interest rate lock and the only thing holding up the closing is your backdating an acknowledgment. If you backdate an acknowledgment in

California, you are committing an act of forgery that can be prosecuted as a felony.

You are encouraged to go back to the signer and notarize the signature properly in order to avoid any hint of wrongdoing. As a matter of course, many notaries do not follow this advice and will simply backdate the acknowledgment and fax it over. You need to know before you are called to do this that it is illegal and is subject to very serious consequences.

**Q. I know there are many ways to take title of a property and different types of documents are often used, such as grant deeds, quitclaim deeds and warranty deeds. How much should I know about property-transfer laws before I notarize these kinds of documents?**

**A.** There are many ways to take title to property, commonly known as "vesting." For example, a husband and wife may choose to vest title as "Joint Tenants" or "Community Property with Rights of Survivorship," or even as "Tenants in Common." Each vesting has serious tax implications, especially upon the death of one or both spouses. As a notary, suggesting a particular vesting for your client can lead to trouble for you later if one member of the couple decides to sue you. Helping a client to fill out the transfer document will only provide additional evidence of your assistance.

From the perspective of the notary, it is not important that you know the differences between vesting options or *taking title*. Remember that you should not provide legal advice or assistance to the document signer(s) and their questions should be redirected to an attorney or their loan officer for clarification.

You should, however, become familiar enough with these types of documents so you recognize who the grantor(s) is/are, so the correct party signs the document. You will also want to ensure that the property's legal description is present prior to notarization.

**Q. There is not enough room on the document for the seal. What should I do?**

**A.** Some documents will have so much text covering the page that even though notary wording is present on the form, there is no room for you to appropriately place your notary seal. Remember that your notary seal must be stamped either below or directly adjacent to your signature which, of course, must be in the immediate proximity of the notary verbiage.

If you do not have enough room for your notary seal on such a page, you must attach a "loose certificate" which will either be an All-Purpose Acknowledgment or a jurat form, depending on the notary act to be performed. Be sure to completely fill out all of the notary verbiage on the loose certificate before you stamp it, since it is always illegal to place your notary seal on any document not containing completed, proper notarial verbiage. Do not, for example, complete and sign the preprinted notary verbiage at the bottom of the form and then place your notary seal in the heading or side margin just because there is space available. Your seal must be in direct proximity to the completed notary wording, and your signature and should be one-quarter inch away for the edge of the paper. If not, the document will most likely be rejected by the county recorder's office.

Of course, in an instance where there is notary verbiage printed but not enough room for the notary stamp, once you have completed and attached the loose certificate, you now have blank notary verbiage left on the original form. You may cross that notary verbiage out with a single diagonal line, and write "see attached acknowledgment" or "see attached jurat," whatever the case may be. Most notaries prefer to fill out this notary verbiage as well as the verbiage on the loose certificate and will simply note somewhere below their signature to reference the acknowledgment or jurat form. This helps anyone reviewing the document to know that the notary did not forget to stamp the document with his or her notary seal.

Every notary has occasionally smudged or smeared their notary stamp on the original document where there was not enough room to properly restamp. Once again, simply treat this occurrence as you would a document with too much text and add your notary seal to a completed loose certificate. Finally, always be sure to attach the loose certificate to the original document with a staple before the client takes it away.

**Q. I have changed my address. Do I need to notify anyone?**

**A.** Whether you change your business address or your residence address, you must notify the secretary of state, per California notary law, by certified mail within 30 days of the change. The secretary of state may need to contact you regarding an inquiry or notary act performed in the past. Without your current address on file, finding you might be difficult. The secretary of state administers significant penalties for notaries failing to comply with this requirement.

**Q. If a document has multiple carbon copies, will the notarization on the original be valid for all copies?**

**A.** Notaries notarize signatures on documents; not the documents. In part, notarization means that the identity of the document signer was verified. This means that a signature must be physically placed onto the document prior to notarization. Even if a document has multiple carbon copies, in order to notarize each copy, the signer must sign the copies individually and the notary's seal, signature, and notary verbiage must be completed on each copy.

**Q. I have heard it is illegal in California to translate the term "notary public" into "notario público" or "notario." Is this true and if so, why?**

**A.** Notaries in other countries have much more legal authority than notaries in the United States. In fact, only attorneys may become notaries in many Latin American countries. Consequently, many people in the United States who immigrated from these countries believe that a notary in the U.S. holds the same legal status as in their respective countries.

As a way to help avoid such confusion, California legislation prohibits the translation of notary public into "notario público" or "notario." The term "notary public" or "notary" can be translated directly into any other language, but not Spanish. Violation of this law can subject the notary to a minimum one-year suspension and possible revocation of their commission.

# ~ CHAPTER 7 ~
# Notarizing In Special Circumstances

**Q. I have been requested by phone to go to a hospital and notarize the signature of a patient. What questions should I ask before I go?**

**A.** Because of the significant potential income available in current markets for notaries who become loan signers, we do not always hear about the experiences of notaries who have chosen to provide services to other markets. One of these markets is hospitals and convalescent centers. You can well imagine the number of documents requiring notarization in these types of public facilities.

As with any other business, you need to know specific information relating to your business in order to be successful. Mobile notary work is no different and many notaries can share experiences of how they have gone on calls only to return home empty handed without even the compensation for gas money spent, not to mention their valuable time. This question, as well as the following question, is included in this book in hopes that it will provide a valuable bit of knowledge before you accept the assignment.

When you receive a call from a hospital or convalescent center, the call will generally come from a patient's relative. He or she will have a document, such as a grant deed transferring the property owned by the patient into his or her name, or another relative's name. In an effort to quickly manage the affairs of the patient before it is too late and everything winds up in probate court, hasty decisions are made and seized upon by a self-appointed overseer.

There is certainly nothing wrong with notarizing documents of this nature and certainly a great service is provided to everyone involved ... usually. However, there are a few questions you should ask before accepting the assignment.

First, you need to find out exactly what form of identification the signer has, since many times the identification especially of elderly patients, is expired well beyond the allowable time limits. If the patient does not have proper identification, you will need to find out if credible witnesses can be used and ensure that the credible witnesses will be present at the same time you are there. There is no time-killer like waiting for a credible witness to arrive from some 40 miles away while you sit there. Also remember that credible witnesses may only be used if they have no direct beneficial or financial interest in the document being notarized.

In other words, if the property transfer is to the benefit of the person who called you, certainly he or she cannot be a credible witness. Sometimes hospital staff will agree to be credible witnesses, but don't count on it. Find out who is to be used and exactly what time he or she will be available.

If there is no proper identification available and no credible witnesses, decline the offer.

Secondly, find out the condition of the patient before you go. If the patient is too sleepy from medication or otherwise not coherent, you will not be able to communicate with that patient and will have to decline the notarization. It is wise, whenever possible, to ask to speak with the patient before accepting the assignment to ensure that your services are being requested by the patient, who will become the document signer (your actual client) rather than the relative who called you. This also helps to ensure that the patient will be expecting you once you arrive.

You can imagine all sorts of scenarios where people, even the adult children of patients, will try to take advantage of the person who is in the facility. Remember who your most important client is: it is the document signer, not the person who requested your services. As long as you are reasonably satisfied that the patient is requesting your services, you are then under obligation to notarize the documents as requested. If the patient is incoherent or lacks the cognitive ability to communicate with you, you will want to decline the notary act, and suggest the family contact an attorney or the ombudsman staff, if available.

Notaries truly walk a fine line when it comes to notarizing documents for someone who they feel may not fully comprehend what he or she is signing. On one hand, laws do not permit notaries to decide whether an individual understands the document being signed or to even decide if someone is being pressured to sign a document. Yet, notaries are people of the highest caliber and do not find it agreeable with their own nature to allow someone to take advantage of a relative's condition.

Speak directly with the patient and make certain that he or she wishes to have his or her signature notarized. If you are not convinced that the patient is making the request, you may decline the notary, regardless of who is paying for your services. If it is clear that the patient wants to have his or her signature notarized, even though you can see that it is a disadvantage to the patient, you are required to notarize the document.

Finally, even before accepting the assignment, provide the caller with your fees before you walk out your front door. Split your fees into two categories: travel and actual notary charges. Depending on your own set rates, you may choose, for example, to charge $60 for travel and the maximum allowable in your state for notary fees. In California the maximum amount you may charge for notary services is $10 per signature notarized. Explain to the person requesting your services over the phone that you will collect the travel fees as soon as you arrive. If you do not take this step and you are forced to decline the notary for a legitimate reason or the patient simply refuses to sign the document, you will have a very difficult time in collecting your travel fees as you leave.

Additionally, you will want to name a fee in case you have to wait for something or someone. Most notaries will charge a certain rate per hour for waiting subdivided into 15-minute increments. Without establishing this over the phone, you may find yourself in the waiting room for hours before being allowed into the room, or you may be waiting at length for a credible witness who was supposed to be "on the way." Your time is worth money, just like everyone else's and you should not wait around for someone without being compensated for that time, regardless of whose fault it is.

Quite often, hospitals and convalescent facilities require that a notary check in with their own staff before going to the patient's room. Check with the staff while you are still on the phone, if possible, and certainly once you arrive at the facility. Following these suggested steps will save you much time as you pursue your mobile notary work.

**Q. I have been asked by phone to go to a jail and notarize the signature of an inmate. What questions should I ask before I go?**

**A.** Jails and prisons are home to many people, and almost everyone there sooner or later needs to have documents notarized. You may receive a call from an attorney or a relative requesting your services. As with the previous question, you need to ask a few questions before accepting the assignment. First, once again, does the signer have proper identification? Find out what type of identification the inmate has and determine whether or not it is acceptable according to your state's laws. If the inmate does not have proper identification, you may need to use credible witnesses, but you must ensure that the credible witnesses do not have a direct beneficial or financial interest in the document to be notarized.

As with the previous question, establish rates over the phone and separate the rates into travel and notary functions. You should definitely consider adding fees for waiting when attending this type of signing, as penal institutions are notoriously slow in summoning the inmate for signings. Again, as with hospitals and convalescent homes, collect the travel fees up front so you will not return empty handed should something not go as expected.

While many states honor verbal contracts, whenever you take an assignment at a hospital, convalescent center or penal institution, you may consider having a prepared contract to fax over for the caller to sign before accepting the assignment. This provides additional protections for you in case of unforeseen circumstances.

# ~ CHAPTER 8 ~
# Power of Attorney Documents

**Q. What is a power of attorney?**

**A.** There are many times when a document must be notarized, but the person who is supposed to sign it cannot be present before a notary at the time of notarization. For example, suppose a husband and wife are purchasing a property, and the documents are scheduled for signature on a day when one of the two is away on a business trip, thus making it impossible for both to appear together before a notary. Certainly, one of the spouses could sign the documents and then the entire document could be mailed to the other spouse for signature, but this takes time and would be inconvenient for everyone involved.

A way around this problem is to have the party who is unavailable for signature and notarization complete a document called a ***power of attorney***. This document gives the authority for one person to enter into a contractual relationship, make decisions or sign documents on behalf of another person. In our example, suppose the wife is away on the business trip and cannot appear before the notary to sign the documents in time for the loan to close. The lender can simply fax over a power of attorney document to the wife, have that document signed before a notary, and have the husband sign the document for his wife.

There are usually two types of power of attorney documents. One is called a ***specific power of attorney***, which specifies what powers the document signer is granting to the other party, and the other is called a ***general power of attorney***. In our previous example, a specific power of attorney would be used only for the specific property and related documents regarding that property or loan for that property.

A general power of attorney, on the other hand, gives a sweeping number of rights enabling another person to represent the grantor's interest in many of the decisions one typically makes for him or herself. For example, suppose someone who is becoming aged chooses to grant all legal decisions to another trusted member of the family or a close friend. That person will then be able to make decisions as he or she determines what is best for the grantor about finances, real estate and a host of other items listed within a general power of attorney.

A power of attorney is a very powerful document, and notaries need to be familiar with it, and how to notarize a document when someone else has been granted these rights.

**Q. How do I notarize a power of attorney signature?**

**A.** This procedure is quite common, as you might imagine, and notaries must be familiar with the proper way to notarize the signer as a power of attorney. We are speaking here of notarizing documents for which a signer is legally signing on behalf of another person. In our previous example, the wife granted power of attorney to her husband. Her husband, therefore has the legal authority to sign documents on behalf of his wife, ***but he does not sign her name***.

Someone who is granted power of attorney is known in the legal community as an "attorney in fact" for the granting party. In our example, the husband is the attorney in fact for his wife. Consequently, every place where his wife would have signed the document, had she been present, he must now sign for her as her attorney in fact. Lets take a look at an example of someone signing as an attorney in fact or with a granted power of attorney.

Suppose John Jones has been granted power of attorney by his wife Cindy Jones to sign documents on her behalf. When the document asks for his wife's signature, since Cindy Jones is unavailable to sign, her husband will sign on her behalf as her attorney in fact, which will be indicated for every location requiring his wife's signature.

*John Jones, attorney in fact for Cindy Jones.*

This is not the only way to sign as attorney in fact. Some lenders may request you to use an alternative style such as:

*Cindy Jones by John Jones as her attorney in fact.*

Whatever the lender requests should be fine as long as it is very clear who was signing the document as attorney in fact and who granted the power of attorney to the signer. Never let the document signer who has been granted power of attorney simply sign the other party's name without the attorney in fact clarification. If you do, the documents will be invalid and rejected, and you could lose your client to another notary.

When entering the information into your official notary journal, you will only be identifying the actual document signer, who in this case is John Jones. When completing the acknowledgment, it is only John Jones who appeared before you and not Cindy Jones, so you will not have any identification information for Cindy Jones. Most notaries will make a note in their journal entry that the document signer signed as attorney in fact, and will name the person who granted the power of attorney as well. This is common practice and should be followed.

# ~ CHAPTER 9 ~
# Certifying Copies of Documents

**Q. What does it mean to "certify a copy" of a document?**

**A.** A certified copy means that the certifying person has examined the original document and the copy, and that the copy is a true and correct duplicate of the original. There are only a few documents that a notary may certify. One is a copy of a power of attorney, as previously indicated, and the other is a copy of the notary's official journal. You may be asked to certify other types of documents, such as academic records, diplomas or birth certificates, but you must decline the request. Certified copies of vital records such as birth certificates must come from the issuing agency; most often the county clerk in the county of birth. Certified copies of academic records are obtained from the institution that originated the records.

As you might imagine, there are times when someone absolutely must certify a document and there is no issuing agency to certify it. Suppose someone wished to certify a copy of a letter. Since the notary cannot certify the letter as it is not on the list of documents a notary is permitted to certify, perhaps there is a way around this problem. A common document used in California is a "Certification by Document Custodian." It requires the document signer to certify the document rather than the notary and the notary can then notarize the signature with a jurat. This document is available on the CD "Essential Notary Forms" at www.notaryclasses.com.

**Q. How do I certify a copy of a power of attorney?**

**A.** Occasionally, a notary may be asked to provide a certified copy of a power of attorney. A certified copy means that the certifying person has examined the original document and the copy, and that the copy is a true and correct duplicate of the original. If someone brings you a copy of a power of attorney to be certified, you must see both the original and the copy for comparison purposes. Most notaries will simply make their own copy and certify that copy, rather than read and compare each word with the original.

State of California

County of ______________

I ________________________(name of notary), Notary Public, certify that on ______________(date), I examined the original power of attorney and the copy of the power of attorney. I further certify that the copy is a true and correct copy of the original power of attorney.

____________________________

Notary Signature

*Sample certification of a power of attorney.*

**Q. Can I notarize a copy of a birth certificate or an academic record?**

**A.** If you perform notary services for the public from an office location you may receive requests to notarize documents such as copies of birth certificates or academic records. Usually, the requesting party will need to send the document to another country that requires the document to be notarized.

The problem here is that a notary in the United States is only guaranteeing certain information about the document signer, not about the document. When another country requires a birth certificate or academic record to be notarized, that country is applying their laws to notaries in the United States. In many countries, once a notary stamps a document, it means that the document was inspected by the notary, and it is an authentic reproduction, or a certified copy. As discussed previously, notaries in the United States do not have the same power or authority as notaries in other countries.

Unfortunately, the person presenting the document before you is in a difficult situation. If you do not notarize the documents, the institution in the country requesting the notarized documents will not accept them, but there is, in effect, nothing for you to notarize. We notarize signatures only. A birth certificate does not have a place for a document signer to sign nor does the academic record or diploma.

For these types of requests, the most common approach is for a notary to use a Copy Certification by Document Custodian. The client (who is for the purposes of this document the document custodian), will sign a statement (certification) which states that the attached document is a true and correct copy of the original. You may then notarize that signature and attach it to the document. You have not violated notary law by notarizing a document that has no place for a signer to place his or her signature and you have not certified the document. It is the client who is stating that the document is a true and correct copy and consequently, the document custodian has certified the document.

Remember if the document is a birth certificate, academic record, a picture or any other kind of document with no means of execution by signature or no verbiage regarding the signer's oath that the content of the document is true, you have nothing to notarize. Since you cannot provide a certified copy of anything other than a power of attorney or your own journal, you will either need to use a Copy Certification by Document Custodian, if requested by the signer, or you must decline the notarization.

**Q. I have been asked to certify a translation of a document from English to Spanish, and I am fluent in Spanish. What should I do?**

**A.** Bilingual notaries are in demand, especially in states where there is a high population of Spanish speakers. If you are bilingual and offer your services to a second language group, you may have requests to certify a translation. ***Notaries, however, do not certify translations.*** When a translation is to be certified, a qualified translator who should know the certification process must complete the translation. His or her signature and statement of certification should be sufficient for most translations, and in some instances, the translator will also need to have his or her signature notarized.

Certifying a translation is really a matter of the qualified translator stating that the translation is accurate. Most of the time, a recognized translation company should be used since the translation company will know the appropriate protocol for certifying the translation.

If you are approached with a request to certify a translation, redirect your client to a translation company or qualified translator. If you are asked to notarize a translation, remember that you must notarize the translation, rather you must notarize the translator's signature stating that he or she is qualified to complete certified translations and that the translation is accurate. Obviously, it will be the translator who needs to appear before you and not the translator's client.

# ~ CHAPTER 10 ~
# Advance Health Care Directives

**Q. What is an advance health care directive?**

**A.** An advance health care directive is a document that states the medical desires of a person should he or she be unable to make those decisions at a later time. Recent events have brought the importance of this document to the forefront of American consciousness. Those who are unwilling to let the medical community make decisions on their behalf, especially in the most extreme conditions have an opportunity to make their wishes known before such a condition arises. Advance health care directives are available in most office-supply stores, and completing these documents has become a priority for many Americans.

These documents specifically list the wishes of the signer for future events, such as whether or not to remain on life support systems or whether or not to donate organs in the event of death. It also lists the person who will be assigned to make the most difficult decisions on a person's behalf, should that person be unable to make those decisions.

If you have read the previous section on power of attorneys, you may wonder if the general power of attorney would not suffice. A general power of attorney grants the authority for someone else to make decisions on one's behalf for just about everything but health care. A power of attorney is not used for making health-care decisions, so if a person wishes to appoint someone to make those kinds of decisions, or wishes to make his or her desires known in the event of a catastrophic condition, an advance health care directive is completed and notarized.

# ~ CHAPTER 11 ~
# Protests

**Q. What is a protest?**

**A.** Notaries are still empowered to "demand payments of bills of exchange and to ***protest*** them in the event of non-payment." This duty is really a carry-over from notarial duties during the 19th century. Briefly, a bill of exchange is a document drawn between parties that one of the parties uses as evidence of money owed. It was a convenient and popular substitute for carrying cash, usually from one county to another. If the party to whom the bill of exchange is presented decides not to honor the payment, it was a notary's duty to formally "demand payment" or "certify the protest" as to why the payment would not be made.

Another example of a notary's function in filing a protest occurred when ships would enter a port with damaged goods. A notary might be called upon to legally verify the damaged goods, seal the written verification and have the document communicated by some means with the cargo's owner or merchant far away.

It is rather unlikely that a notary today would be asked to provide such a service. If presented with such a request, the notary should not proceed unless under the direction of an attorney.

# ~ CHAPTER 12 ~
# Notary Seals

**Q. I have noticed that most notary seals are black. Is black the only color allowed?**

**A.** While some states do require the notary seal to be a specific color, in California a notary seal or stamp can be any color so long as it is photographically reproducible. If you are the type who likes creativity and to be a little different, this is one area in which you might decide to not express your creative side. California county recorders are used to seeing black-inked notary seals, and you do not want to give any reason for someone to reject a document even if it is for an illegitimate reason.

**Q. I have notarized a document but the seal smeared a bit during the process. Should I reseal it?**

**A.** Never hand a document back to your client if the notary seal is smudged or not perfectly legible. The county recorder will most likely reject the document and require re-notarization. This could cost the client a lot of time and possibly money, not just for the re-notarization process. Rate locks are time-sensitive, and loans must close by specific times or the rate lock could be lost. At the least, everyone will be inconvenienced and you may find you have lost a good client for future business.

If you do not have enough room on the document to re-notarize, simply attach a loose acknowledgment or jurat that is properly completed and sealed.

# ~ CHAPTER 13 ~
# Notary Journals

**Q. Can you give me step-by-step instructions for filling out a journal entry?**

**A.** Every notary act performed requires a journal entry and for new notaries, completing the first few entries can be a daunting task. What is to be included and where? It becomes especially confusing when using one or two credible witnesses. As with any other task, once you learn how to do it, the task is easy. For first timers, any help is appreciated.

There are a wide number of journals from which to choose, but every journal, regardless of organization, will have similar entries. The entries may appear in a different order, but notary law requires that certain information be entered into a journal. For your convenience, a typical journal entry sample is reprinted below. You will notice a left page and a right page that go together to make up one single journal entry.

**Step-by-Step Instructions for Journal Entries:**

1. Every journal entry requires the date and time of notarization. Many notaries do not realize the importance of including the time in their record, but this is a legal requirement and smart practice anyway. Notice that in this journal entry, the date is abbreviated, but is not entirely numerical. There is no requirement regarding formatting of dates, but you may find it advantageous for legibility among other reasons to at least abbreviate the month. Similarly, you may notice that the time is noted as military time or in 24-hour notation. Again, while not

required, using this format helps to eliminate confusion if the record needs to be evaluated at a later time.

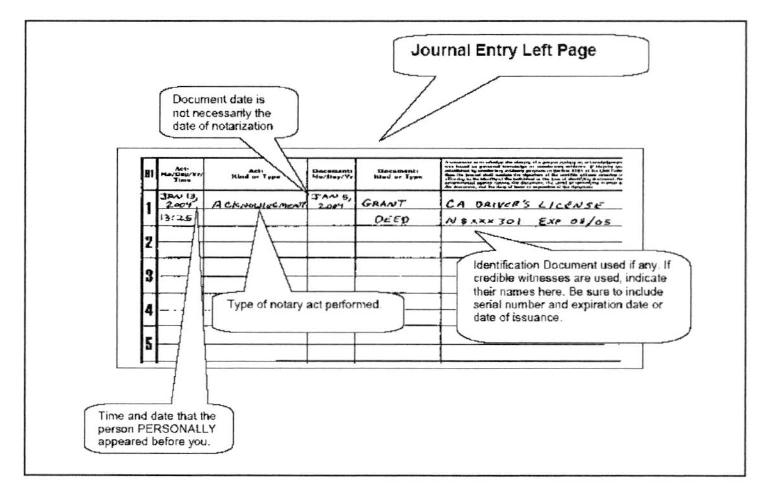


2. You must indicate what type of notary act was performed. This will usually be an acknowledgment or a jurat as these two services make up 99 percent of all notary services for most notaries. Other notary acts may include responding to the secretary of state, providing a certified copy of a journal entry and so on. When you enter in the type of notary act, try to keep consistent each time. For example, if you want to abbreviate "acknowledgment" with "ack," use that abbreviation for each entry for which an acknowledgment was completed.

3. In this particular journal, we next find an entry for the document date. Since this information is not legally required, it is not necessarily included in every type of journal. The document date is not necessarily the date the notary was completed. Remember, for example, that documents requiring an acknowledgment may be signed prior to the day of notarization as long as the signer appears before the notary and acknowledges to the notary that the signature is indeed his or hers. Almost every document you notarize will have a document date somewhere on it. Enter that date in this location.

4. The next item to be entered in this particular journal is the name or title of the document notarized. In the case of our example, the document was a grant deed. Entering this information is a legal requirement. A word of caution to loan signers regarding this point: you should not simply put a description such as "loan docs" in this area. You should individually list each document that you are notarizing. While this is not common practice, individual listings will help to provide you with evidence of exactly what you notarized. This can be critical should your client raise a question later about which documents were notarized.
5. Next, you will need to provide the information you used to properly identify the document signer. If you are using an identification document such as a driver's license, you will need the serial number of the identification document (driver's license number), the expiration date or the date of issue of the identification document, and a description of the identification document. If you are not using an identification document because you personally know the document signer, then simply indicate in this section "personal knowledge" and move on.
6. In our journal example, the next page begins with the address of the document signer. While this information is not required, including it may assist someone in locating the signer at a later time if needed. The address does not necessarily have to match the address on the identification document. Many people move without changing the address on their driver's licenses for months. Ask the client if the address provided is a current address, and record.
7. Every document notarized will require the signature of the signer in your journal at the time of notarization. This signature should reasonably match the signature on the document notarized, as well as the signature on the identification document. People's signatures often change significantly over the years, but not usually so much that you cannot

reasonably ascertain whether or not the signature on the document and in your journal are a close-enough match with the signature on the identification. If the signature cannot be reasonably matched, you may need to use a different form of identity or perhaps even question whether or not the signer is really the person named within the document.

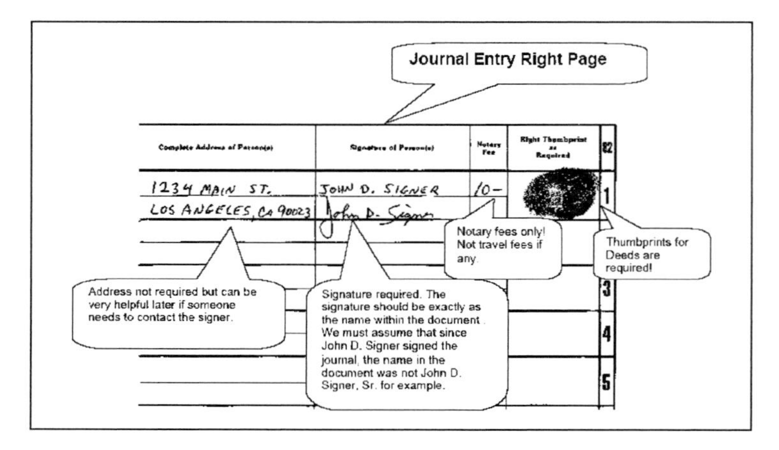


If someone does commit forgery by signing someone else's name, but the identification card still matches the person and the forgery is done well enough that the average person could not know, then the notary will not be held responsible should that person be caught later. The notary is held responsible if he or she commits an illegal action or if he or she is negligent. If a notary performs his or her responsibilities dutifully and someone else commits an illegal action without the notary's knowledge, it is extremely unlikely that a notary will be subject to prosecution or punitive measures. Check signatures carefully and follow the requirements, and you should never have a problem.

8. You may notice in our journal example that the name is also printed above the signature. Many signatures are somewhat illegible, so you should always have the signer print his or her name legibly above the signature in your journal. Furthermore, the printed name should always match the name on the

document notarized. If the signature matches the identification document, even if it is illegible, you should accept that signature. The signer may or may not be required to print his or her name on the document underneath the illegible signature. Most loan-signing documents will already have the name preprinted for this reason.

9. Finally, you will notice a thumbprint in the journal. Notaries take thumbprints for just about everything notarized, but doing so is not required for all, except a few types of documents. Documents that transfer property such as grant deeds or quitclaim deeds do require a right thumbprint. Thumbprints are also required on documents that place properties into collateral for securing a property loan such as we find with a deed of trust or a security agreement.

   By the way, if the right thumbprint is unavailable, use the left thumb. Otherwise, use any available finger and be sure to identify which finger was used in your journal and an explanation as to why it was used (i.e. right index finger, signer missing both thumbs). If no prints are available because of missing or deformed hands, simply record in your journal as to the condition. Make certain that your client's thumbprint is of the entire thumb area and not just the tip. This may become critical information should an investigation into the identity of the signer later ensue.

**Q. A law enforcement official has presented me with a subpoena for my notary journals. Does this mean I have to turn over the originals or copies?**

**A.** If a member of law enforcement requests your journals, you will need to turn over your original journals. The officer must present you with a subpoena or court order for your journals and must also provide you with a receipt for the journals. Be sure the receipt includes the period of journal entries which were handed over, as well as the contact information of the officer taking the journals.

You must then send a certified letter to the secretary of state within 10 days indicating that the journals were turned over in accordance with the subpoena. You will need to include your name, commission number, expiration of your commission, and the period of journal entries which were turned over.

If the subpoena merely requires copies of the journal, you must be present during the copying procedure and you must certify those copies if requested to do so. In this case, since you will be keeping the actual journals, the secretary of state will not need to be notified.

**Q. I became a notary for a job and the employer paid for everything, including the journal and seal. I am now leaving and the employer is demanding that I leave both the journal and the seal. Should I at least keep copies of the journal?**

**A.** When the notary who has obtained a commission as an employee leaves the employer, he or she is to keep his or her notary seal and journals. The employer may not demand that neither the notary seal nor the journal be returned to them or left on their premises after termination of employment. Remember that the commission is yours; the seal and journal are your personal property which you must retain and control at all times. If your employer wishes to have copies of the notary journal records pertaining to the business, you must supervise the process of copying.

On a related note regarding employment, if, during the course of your commission, your place of business changes, you will need to notify the secretary of state by certified mail within 30 days of your new business address. You will not need to refile your oath or bond if your place of business is in a different county, unless you wish to do so. If so, you will have 30 days to obtain a new notary seal for the new county.

As an employee, if your position is terminated or you resign prior to the expiration date of your commission, your commission does not automatically expire unless you are commissioned on behalf of the state, city, county, or public school districts, or on behalf of a military installation. If this is the case, you must resign your commission when you terminate employment. If you elect to resign your commission after changing employment, you must notify the secretary of state in writing, and turn in all notary journals to the county clerk's office within 30 days.

**Q. Do I have to take a right thumbprint for everything I notarize?**

**A.** A right thumbprint is required for deeds such as warranty deeds, quitclaim deeds, grant deeds or deeds of trust affecting real property. Please note that not all documents containing the word deed in their title require a right thumbprint! For example, thumbprints are not required for deeds of reconveyance or for a trustee's deed if the property is in foreclosure. (When a property loan is paid in full, a deed of reconveyance is issued; a trustee's deed is issued for transfer of property that has been placed into foreclosure.)

# ~ CHAPTER 14 ~
# Lost or Stolen Journals and Notary Seals

**Q. I have lost a few of my notary journals. Do I need to notify anyone?**

**A.** If the journal is stolen, lost, destroyed, damaged, or otherwise rendered unusable, the notary public must immediately notify the secretary of state by certified or registered mail. The notification must include:

1. The period of the journal entries;
2. The notary public commission number;
3. The expiration date of the commission;
4. When applicable, a photocopy of any police report that may have been taken.

**Q. I have lost my seal and need to obtain another ASAP. What should I do?**

**A.** If the official seal is lost, destroyed, or damaged, you will need to contact the secretary of state through certified mail. A new certificate of authorization will be issued upon request within five working days after receipt of the notice. You may then use this authorization form to obtain a replacement seal. You will mail this new authorization to an approved notary seal manufacturer who will make and send your replacement notary seal. Once your notary commission is expired, you must destroy the seal to prevent possible fraudulent use by another.

# ~ CHAPTER 15 ~
# Identifying the Signer

**Q. What is an "identification document"?**

**A.** If a notary does not personally know the document signer, he or she must prove his or her identity to the notary by an acceptable form of identification. A printed form of identification is commonly referred to as an ***identification document***. Credible witnesses may also be used for identification purposes. They would not be referred to as an "identification document," since credible witnesses are people who claim personal knowledge of the document signer's identity.

**Q. What identification documents are permissible for notarizing signatures?**

**A.** Most states, including California, permit the following:

1. An identification card or driver's license issued by the Department of Motor Vehicles which is current or has been issued within the past five years.
2. A passport issued by the Department of State of the United States which is current or has been issued within the past five years.
3. Any one of the following, as long as it is current or has been issued within five years, and contains a photograph and description of the person named on it and is signed by the person. It ***must*** bear a serial or other identifying number. If the document is a foreign passport, the United States Citizenship and Immigration Services must have stamped it. (The USCIS stamp is adequate to meet this requirement.)
   a. A passport issued by a foreign government.

b. A driver's license issued by any state or by a Canadian or Mexican public agency authorized to issue drivers' licenses.
c. An identification card issued by any state motor vehicles department.
d. An identification card issued by any branch of the armed forces of the United States.
e. An inmate identification card issued on or after January 1, 1988, by the Department of Corrections, if the inmate is in custody. (Not an ID bracelet.)

Remember a signer's identification document must contain at least as much information as contained in the signature, which should match the document. For example, when notarizing the signature for John Smith Jr., the "Jr." must also appear on the identification document. ***The identification document can contain more information than the signature, but never less.*** If someone signs the document as Mary Ann Smith and her driver's license only has Mary Smith, you must use an alternate form of identification that has her name in the form of Mary Ann Smith. Similarly, John W. Jones II must have an identification document with at least John W. Jones II.

**Q. What if the document signer recently changed his or her name through marriage, but has no identification documents reflecting the new name. Should he or she sign with the old name instead?**

**A.** This is a very common problem, especially for loan signers. The documents will be drawn up in her new name, but the identification is still in his or her former name. If you cannot obtain an acceptable form of identification and the document cannot be changed by its originator to reflect the name for which identification is given, you will either have to suggest he or she use a notary whom she or she personally knows or you will need to use credible witnesses in order to proceed. You may not use a marriage certificate to prove the name change.

**Q. Am I allowed to use an expired driver's license for identification?**

**A.** As long as an identification document has been issued within the past five years, you may use it as an approved form of ID. Most drivers' licenses, for example, will have a date of issuance printed on the bottom or the reverse side of the card.

**Q. What if someone used a falsified driver's license and I notarized the document without that knowledge. Will I be held responsible for negligence?**

**A.** If someone does commit forgery by signing someone else's name but the identification card still matches the person and the forgery is done well enough that the average person could not know, then the notary will not be held responsible should that person be caught later.

The notary is held responsible if he or she commits an illegal action or if he or she is negligent. If a notary performs his or her responsibilities dutifully and someone else commits an illegal action without the notary's knowledge, it is extremely unlikely that the notary will be subject to prosecution or punitive measures. Check signatures carefully and follow the requirements and you should never have a problem.

**Q. Is it my responsibility to confirm the authenticity of an identification document?**

**A.** If an identification document is obviously a fake, clearly your responsibility as a notary is to reject that form of identification. You may even consider it a moral obligation to report the false ID to the authorities for further action. If you have a concern about the authenticity of an identification document—if it looks as if it has been tampered with—but you are unsure, you should request another form of identification.

Remember that the notary verbiage states that the document signer proved his or her identity to you, so if you are not convinced of the identity, use another form of ID. If no other form of identification is available, you may use credible witnesses and if those are unavailable, you will need to decline the notary procedure until acceptable identification can be presented. However, it is not your obligation to confirm the authenticity of the identification document, as such a task would virtually be an impossible one.

**Q. Can I notarize a document for someone who does not have any forms of identification?**

**A.** If a client cannot present an approved form of identification, you may use the credible witness procedure for identification. This procedure is described in detail later in this book. Of course, if you personally know the client, identification documents are not even required. California allows the use of two credible witnesses when necessary.

**Q. Is an international driver's license acceptable as proof of identification?**

**A.** You should never accept an international driver's license as proof of identification. While there are legitimate international driver's licenses, these can also be obtained through the Internet with no verification of identity. Also, you should note that Social Security cards cannot be used, since they do not meet the above-listed criteria, nor should credit cards be used even if they do have a picture of the person.

**Q. Can I use a Social Security card or birth certificate as identification?**

**A.** An acceptable identification must contain a photograph and signature of the person, among the other criteria mentioned previously. Since Social Security cards and birth certificates have neither the photograph nor the signature, neither one may be used for identification when notarizing documents. This leaves me to believe that if I find an ID that is current, has a picture, signature, description and identification number, such as an employee ID care, it would be OK to use it. You may want to reiterate that the ID must be on the approved list from the office of the secretary of state.

# ~ CHAPTER 16 ~
# Using Credible Witnesses

**Q. What is a "credible witness"?**

**A.** If someone requiring notarial services lacks the proper identification, we can use a procedure called "obtaining a credible witness." A credible witness must personally know the signer and be personally known by the notary. In addition, the credible witness must swear an oath or affirmation to the notary that the person making the acknowledgment is the person named within the document.

A credible witness may be used only if all of the following requirements are met:

1. The credible witness personally knows the person making the acknowledgment.
2. It is the reasonable belief of the witness that the circumstances of the person making the acknowledgment are such that it would be very difficult or impossible for that person to obtain another form of identification.
3. The person making the acknowledgment does not possess any of the identification documents named earlier.
4. The witness does not have a financial interest in the document being acknowledged and is not named in the document.

**Q. When must I use two credible witnesses?**

**A.** In California, if the credible witness does not know the notary or if the notary does not know the credible witness, then two credible witnesses may be used whose identities are proven to the notary. Please note that credible witnesses may not have any financial interest in the document, nor may they be named within the document. Most states do not allow the use of two credible witnesses.

**Q. How do I find credible witnesses?**

**A.** When you are in the field, it is not always easy to quickly locate credible witnesses when you need them. The quickest approach is to ask the client if any neighbors or relatives would be willing to come over and be credible witnesses. Of course, many clients will hesitate, since most people prefer to keep personal affairs as private as possible.

**Q. Can I use a single credible witness if two cannot be found?**

**A.** Unfortunately, unless you as the notary personally know a credible witness, you must find two or reschedule the signing until two are available.

**Q. How do I record the credible witness information in the journal?**

**A.** The credible witness(s) do not sign the document but must sign the notary journal. Remember that a single credible witness must personally be known by the notary and must personally know the signer, so the notary will not use identification documents to verify identity. However, with two credible witnesses, identification documents are used, since the notary does not personally know either credible witness. Of course, if the notary knew either one of the credible witnesses, only one would be required.

When recording credible witnesses into your journal, keep in mind that the credible witnesses are really the means of identification for the document signer. Instead of using a driver's license or passport for identification, you are accepting the word of another individual or individuals that he or she knows the document signer. When you do use a credible witness, notate in your journal in the location where you would normally put the identification document information—such as driver's license number and expiration date—the words "credible witness, see below." Now, just below in the next lines for a new record entry, put the information for the credible witnesses and have each one sign the journal. You do not have to get their right thumbprint, but as common practice, most notaries obtain one thumbprint anyway. People are more hesitant to commit perjury or fraud if they know that a formal record, including a thumbprint, will be retained.

**Q. Can a minor be used as a credible witness?**

**A.** Some states prohibit the use of anyone under 18 years of age to be used as a credible witness and in general, even if your state does not, you should consider adopting this policy. Using a minor is just is not a good idea, period. Should a document ever wind up in court and you used a 10-year-old as a credible witness, there might be cause for complaint and your notary practices may be under serious question.

# ~ CHAPTER 17 ~
# Signature by Mark Procedures

**Q. What does "signature by mark" mean?**

**A.** If the signer of a document cannot write (sign) his or her name, that person may sign by the mark "x." The requirements for signature by mark are as follows:

Two persons who can write their own names as witnesses on the document must witness the signer's mark. Neither of these persons has to know the document signer, they only have to witness the document signing. One witness should write the person's name next to the person's mark, and then the witness should sign his or her name as a witness. The witnesses are only verifying that they witnessed the individual make his or her mark on the signature line of the document. A notary public is not required to identify the two persons who witnessed the signing by mark or to have the two witnesses sign the journal.

**Q. Where and how do the two witnesses sign when completing a signature by mark?**

**A.** Take a look at the example of a document signed by John Smith, who could not write his name. He signed with an "x." His friend Mary Jones wrote his name, John Smith, for him next to the mark and then signed as well. Finally Peter R. Roberts, another acquaintance of John Smith, also signed his name as a witness.

Date: August 18, 2005 Name: X John Smith by: Mary Jones (Witness #1)

Peter R. Roberts (Witness #2)

You can easily see here that Mary Jones signed John Smith after Mr. Smith placed his mark (x) on the document. Peter R. Roberts signs as a witness but does not need to resign Mr. Smith's name.

**Q. How is an individual identified if they have used a mark for their signature?**

**A.** It is important to note that when you perform a notarization for a person who is signing by mark, you must still verify the identity of the person signing by mark, In addition, you must have that person also sign the journal with his or her mark. That person must also sign under his or her own power. It may be acceptable for someone to support his or her arm during the signing, but the notary cannot allow the person helping to make the mark or signature for the person by guiding the signer's hand.

Identifying an individual who is signing by mark is not always so easy. We usually compare signatures and physical descriptions against an identification document, but if someone had a stroke for example and can no longer sign with his or her usual signature, the identification document no longer serves the purpose. At this point, we have no choice but to use one or two credible witnesses.

While those who witness the signing by mark may or may not have personally known the document signer and may or may not have been named within the document, credible witnesses of course must know the document signer personally and may not have a beneficial or financial interest in the document being notarized.

**Q. How do I enter information into the journal if I used two witnesses with a signature by mark procedure?**

**A.** Since the signature by mark witnesses do not need to sign the journal, simply record the information for the notary act as you normally would and have the signer sign with his or her mark in your journal. Of course, if you need to use credible witnesses for identification, you would then complete their information in your journal as well and have each credible witness sign your journal. See the discussion in the previous chapter on using credible witnesses for additional procedural information, if necessary.

# ~ CHAPTER 18 ~
# Unusual Requests

**Q. I have been asked to notarize a will. Are there any special procedures to follow?**

**A.** If you are asked to notarize a will, you should decline unless an attorney requests the notarization. Some wills will be negated if anyone else, including the notary, signs the document. As a notary, you would not be expected to know whether or not a particular will would be negated with your signature, but you simply need to refer the client to an attorney who handles wills and estates.

**Q. I have an affidavit which purports to identify the document signer. May I notarize this document and if so, how?**

**A.** If the wording of a document purports to identify an affiant (signer of a written affidavit), and the document includes the birthdate or age of the person and a photograph or thumbprint of the person, the notary must require a certified copy of the person's birth certificate, an identification card or a DMV-issued license. If the form is required for immigration purposes, the notary may accept identification documents acceptable to the United States Citizenship and Immigration Services.

**Q. What does it mean when a client is required to have the notary's signature certified?**

**A.** Sometimes, a client will present to you a document that requires notarization, and following notarization, needs to have your signature certified. When you file your oath with the county clerk in the county that is to be your primary place of business, your signature will be on file. If a client needs to have your signature certified, the document you notarized will need to be presented to the county clerk's office where your signature is on file. The county clerk has staff that handles these kinds of notary requirements.

Once you notarize the document for your client, the client will need to present it to the county clerk staff and request the notary certification. The county clerk will compare your signature on file with your signature on the notarized document, and provide the client with a separate document of certification.

The client will always know which county clerk to go to since the county appears on your notary seal.

**Q. What is an "apostille"?**

**A.** There are many documents that require notarization prior to sending them to a foreign country. Since 1981, the United States has been part of an agreement between other countries referred to as the 1961 Hague Convention. In part, this means that the participating countries do not need to require "Legalization of Foreign Documents" as long as specific procedures are followed. When a document is notarized, the document must first be presented to the county clerk for certification of the notary's signature. In this case, the document must be executed in the county where the notary has filed his or her oath.

Once certified, the client must forward the document to an agency within the state that is responsible for completing the apostille. The county clerk will have information on addresses for completing this process.

Once the apostille is added to the document, it will be recognized by any other country who is also part of the Hague Convention, thereby eliminating the arduous steps in having a document formally legalized. Although it appears to be a complicated procedure, it really is nothing more than a bit time consuming, and is a wonderful convenience for anyone needing to send formal documents to foreign countries.

Many of the documents that require an apostille are those which you would not typically notarize. For example, marriage licenses, birth certificates, academic records and so on.

Since these kinds of documents do not have a place for the document signer to sign, many states, including California, allow the use of a Copy Certification by Document Custodian.

This document requires the signer to certify that the copies presented before you are true and correct. You may notarize this document, attach it to the copy, and then send the signer to the county clerk where you have your oath and bond on file in order to complete the apostille process.

**Q. Can I notarize a document for a minor?**

**A.** Individuals under the age of 18 who are not emancipated in general cannot legally enter into contracts, but occasionally, you may be requested to notarize a document for someone underage. A notary may notarize documents for a minor as long as the identification for the minor meets the criteria set forth for adults, or the notary personally knows the minor. While minors under 15 would not typically have a valid driver's license, many do have passports. It is a good practice to also note the age of the minor in your journal. Most notaries will also attempt to ensure that the minor understands the document he or she is signing before notarizing.

# ~ CHAPTER 19 ~
# Subscribing Witnesses

**Q. What is a "subscribing witness"?**

**A.** When a person has signed or wishes to sign a document but cannot personally appear before a notary, the signer can request another person to sign the document as a witness to the principal signer's signature and have the document notarized. That person is called a "subscribing witness." The subscribing witness must either witness the document signer signing the document, or have the document signer acknowledge that he or she did sign the document.

The subscribing witness must personally know the identity of the document signer and the notary public must personally know the subscribing witness. If the notary does not personally know the subscribing witness, then his or her identity must be established, or proved, by a third party who personally knows the subscribing witness and is personally known by the notary public. That third party is called a credible witness.

The subscribing witness must swear under oath that he or she either saw the principal sign the document or heard the signer acknowledge that he or she signed it, and that the signer requested him or her to sign the document as a witness.

The subscribing witness must sign the document as well as the notary's official journal. In addition, if the subscribing witness was identified by a credible witness, then the credible witness must also sign the notary's official journal. Notice that the credible witness only signs the journal and not the document, whereas the subscribing witness must sign both.

**Q. Can a subscribing witness be used to notarize any document?**

**A.** A subscribing witness cannot be used in conjunction with any deed of trust, mortgage, security agreement, quitclaim deed, or grant deed document.

Most notaries will never have a request for completing a "Proof of Execution." If you are asked to perform this function, be sure that you understand it first.

Although is sounds complicated, in reality, the procedure is simple.

1. The document signer signs the document in front of someone he or she knows personally or tells that person that he or she signed the document.
2. The signer requests the person to sign the document as a "witness."
3. The witness then takes the document to a notary who knows him or her personally or finds another person who knows him or her and is known personally by a notary.
4. The witness must swear an oath to the notary that he or she either saw the signer sign the document or that fact was acknowledged to him or her by the signer and that the signer asked him or her to sign the document as a witness.
5. The witness proves the identity of the document signer based on personal knowledge.
6. The notary completes the Subscribing Witness Jurat.

**SUBSCRIBING WITNESS JURAT**

State of ____________ }
County of ____________ } ss.

This form is used for a Subscribing Witness. The notary act is known as a "Proof of Execution."

On ____________ (date) before me, the undersigned, a notary public for the state, personally appeared ____________ (subscribing witness's name) ☐ personally known to me or ☐ proved to me (on the oath of ____________ (credible witness's name), who is personally known to me) to be the person whose name is subscribed to the within instrument, as a witness thereto, who, being by me duly sworn, deposed and said that he/she was present and saw/heard acknowledged

____________ (name[s] of principal[s])

the same person(s) described in and whose name(s) is/are subscribed to the within and annexed instrument in his/her/their authorized capacity(ies) as (a) party (ies) thereto, execute the same, and that said affiant subscribed his/her name to the within instrument as a witness at the request of

____________ (name[s] of principal[s]).

WITNESS my hand and official seal.

____________
Notary Signature

OPTIONAL INFORMATION

While law does not require the following information, completing relevant portions may minimize the potential of this document being fraudulently attached to another document subsequent to signing.

____________
Name of document

____________
Date of document

____________
Number of pages

____________
Other information

A-4

*Subscribing Witness Jurat.*

# ~ CHAPTER 20 ~
# How Do I Make Money?

**Q. How much money can a notary public really make?**

**A.** The industry appeal for new notary publics is that there is exceptional income potential without investing much more than a few hundred dollars and hard work to get started. There are very few business opportunities that match the convenience and the level of income as with becoming a notary public. Notaries who are new in the field have as much an opportunity of being successful as longtime notaries.

How much money can a notary public make? Notaries who work for an employer rarely see much additional income as the notary service simply becomes part of their job function. Occasionally the employer will recognize the value of having a notary available for the company or their clients and increase the salary of the notary. Notaries are encouraged to speak with their employers about such a possible increase. Remember that even though you may be working as a notary for an employer, you are still personally held liable for your notarial work. Taking on this liability should be worth additional money to your employer if you bring this to their attention.

Notaries who want to earn a substantial income start their own business as a mobile notary and especially as a loan signer. The typical fee for attending a loan signing as a notary is between $50 and $150. Some companies do pay over $200, but this is not the average.

Suppose you gain some experience and several clients who are lending companies, title companies or loan-signing companies and your rates average $90 per loan signing. (By the way, within a year you should be averaging over $100 per loan.) Now suppose you decided to work a schedule of only three loans per day for five days a week. It takes on average one hour per loan, with one hour drive time and one-half hour preparation, so each loan would take on average 2.5 hours. Your workday for this schedule is 7.5 hours. Seasoned loan signers will tell you that these numbers are quite conservative and successful loan signers are able to do much better than this. Nevertheless, it is important that you have a realistic goal.

Under this schedule you will have earned $270 per day or $1,350 per week. Suppose you only decided to work this schedule every other week. In other words, you work one week and take the next one off. Factoring this into the equation also provides you with time to market your services to additional clients. At $1,350 per week for 26 weeks, your income is $35,100 for the year. On a regular-paid job you would need to earn $27 per hour, work 40 hours per week and work the entire 52 weeks in the year (less paid vacations) to earn the same money.

An aggressive, successful loan signer can earn well over $100,000 per year and there are many who do just that. Even though there is a high income potential for notaries who are loan signers, loan signers who do not want to commit to as much time as the most successful loan-signers can make very respectable incomes and have as much personal time off as they wish. You can easily see why people want to explore the opportunities of notaries and loan signers.

**Q. What is a loan signer?**

**A.** Most notaries work for themselves by starting their own notary business. The most lucrative has always been in the loan-signing market. A loan signer is a notary who specializes in notarizing loan documents. While not a legal requirement, becoming successful in the loan-signing business requires knowledge about the lending industry and the most common loan documents. If you are a new notary and want to take advantage of the loan-signing opportunities, you should consider taking a one-day loan-signing class, which will help to prepare you before you take your first loan-signing assignment.

The class will discuss marketing opportunities and strategies as well as typical loan-signing documents you will see in the field. Some loan-signing classes even have an extra option of riding along with a loan signer on an actual assignment.

Whether you have taken a loan-signing class or want to take one, this kind of option is one of the most valuable ways of gaining experience in a hands-on environment. In California, contact www.notaryclasses.com or call (800) 873-9865 if you are interested in this valuable experience.

**Q. Do I have to be a notary to become a loan signer?**

**A.** All loan signers must also be commissioned notaries. Your function is to notarize loan documents for the document signer.

**Q. What is the difference between a loan signer and a certified loan signer?**

**A.** Notaries who become loan signers almost always become certified by a recognized certification program such as the one offered by www.notaryclasses.com or the National Notary Association. There is no legal requirement to become a certified loan signer, but not being certified definitely limits your opportunities. In fact, most loan signers choose to become certified with a number of different companies, as each one provides different opportunities within the loan-signing industry.

**Q. What is AP Certification?**

**A.** AP Certification is granted from the Association of Professional Notaries and Certified Signing Agents. You can find out more information about the benefits of this association at www.notaryclasses.com.

**Q. What is the National Notary Association?**

**A.** The National Notary Association is widely recognized as one of the oldest associations for notaries in the United States. If you are a new notary and are considering joining several associations, this one is certainly worth considering, even though the programs offered are usually quite expensive compared to other companies.

**Q. How can I market myself as a notary or loan signer?**

**A.** The keys to success in any business is a combination of good service and consistent marketing. As a new loan signer or mobile notary you have many proven ways of marketing, most of which take much more time than money. If you are a new loan signer, consider signing up with a minimum of 100 companies as soon as possible. These can be loan-signing companies, lenders and title companies in your area, and escrow companies. Too many new notaries stop marketing too early. As with any other business, the phone will not stay busy if you only let a few people know about your services. Broadcast to everyone you can.

You should definitely consider signing up on sites like www.thenotarylist.com, www.notaryrotary.com, www.123notary.com, and the National Notary Association at www.nationalnotary.org. These sites are accessed by lending and escrow companies all over the United States, and can be a very valuable resource for notaries, especially those just starting in the business.

Some loan-signing books like ***How to Become a Wildly Successful Loan Signer***, available at www.notaryclasses.com, take you through the entire process of marketing, including how to structure your contacts, when to make personal contacts and how to follow up with potential business leads. There are even suggestions on how to market yourself by offering services that most loan signers never think of, but could be wonderfully valuable.

Never forget that success in any business requires consistent effort at least until your client base is established. Most successful loan signers have around 10 clients who use them frequently so if you are only working with three or four, start marketing right away. Send out your flyers or better yet, take your information personally to prospective clients. Do not stop until you have made contact with no less than 100 potential clients. Following these guidelines is the recommendation for gaining a solid market share as a new loan signer.

**Q. I do not want to become a loan signer, but I still want to have my own notary business. Is this possible?**

**A.** Certainly not every notary becomes a loan signer. There is a market for notaries who are not loan signers. These notaries provide much needed services for hospitals, convalescent centers, retirement centers, jails and prisons, just to name a few. Most notaries begin their business by purchasing an ad in the Yellow Pages and passing out informational flyers to the local facilities requiring notary services. Just about everyone needs a notary sooner or later and most people need notaries many different times throughout life. If you do not feel comfortable starting off as a loan signer, consider becoming a mobile notary. Find out what to charge by investigating typical notary rates in your area and setting yours according to your own value of time. You do not have to be the lowest-charging notary out there to get business. When someone needs a notary the need is usually immediate and $10 or $20 differences between notaries will not usually be the deciding factor. Most of the time, it is the notary who answers the phone who will be requested, as long as the pricing is reasonable.

Finally, if you have read Chapter 1 in this book you know that you already have a potential client base of hundreds, even thousands, of people, but you must let them know about your services. Almost everyone needs a notary sooner or later and word of mouth is without question the very best form of advertising. If you have not read Chapter 1, chances are that you have not read the rest of this book either. Read this book before you accept your first assignment, please! No one should begin a business before he or she has learned as much as possible about the business. There is so much information covered in this book that you could not possibly learn in a one-day notary class or a home study, and chances are that whatever you learned for the test you will have forgotten much of it by the time your commission is sent.

## L



## M



## N



## O



## P



## S